The Job Interview
MASTER

by Doug A Stowell

ISBN: 146091726X
ISBN-13: 9781460917268

FOREWORD

Welcome to *The Job Interview Master* and thank you for putting your faith in this book!

Purchasing this book indicates that you are serious about your interviews. We want to give you the best opportunity possible to stand out from the competition.

Lessons from thousands of interviews conducted by the contributors are condensed here into this book.

The Job Interview Master is a collection of the toughest and most common interview questions you can expect to be asked.

We want to familiarize you with the toughest questions that consistently come up in interviews in one form or another. In this book we outline 150 of these questions and we split them cross 8 categories.

We break down each question into what is actually being asked and what is expected in return. More often than not, there are hidden meanings in questions and this is what you need to be aware of.

All interview questions are analyzed within this book and three unique answers provided for each by seasoned interviewers.

We want you to think about each answer. Apply it to your situation and industry and formulate an answer or answers that utilizes the tips we provide.

The contributors to this book have recruited for Wall Street, Retail, Pharmaceutical, Consulting, Construction, Engineering and many other industries.

The Job Interview Master is industry neutral and applies to a cross section of job candidates.

Interviews can be very nerve wracking for many reasons but quite often the anticipation is worse than reality. The more you are prepared, the better your chances! Remember, preparedness means anticipating the questions and having your answers ready.

Win the interviewer over by learning to give answers that show that you really understand the implied questions.

So let's get going!

The best of luck,
Doug A Stowell.

ACKNOWLEDGEMENTS

I would like to thank all the professionals who contributed to this book, for their time and patience in trying to help others overcome interview nerves. A special thanks to Pauline for her never ending understanding and love!

TABLE OF CONTENTS

CHAPTER 1: ALL ABOUT YOU 1

Introduction 1

What has been your biggest failure? 2

How would your best friend describe you? 3

What is the toughest decision you have ever made? 4

What is your best idea to date? 5

What has been your biggest success? 6

What would you have done differently if you started your work life again? 7

What are the most important rewards you expect gain from your career? 8

Sell me your shoes in 1 minute. 9

If you won the lottery tomorrow would you still work? 10

What is the ideal role for you? 11

What are your three strongest points? 12

What are your weakest points? 13

What makes you get out of bed in the morning? 14

How do you rate your communication skills? 15

What are your main goals? 16

Do you consider yourself lucky? 17

Do you have a personal mission statement? 18

What is your measure of success? 19

Where do you see yourself in a number of years? 20

How strong are your analytical skills? 21

Have you done your best work yet? 22

CHAPTER 2: YOUR CAREER TO DATE 25

Introduction 25

At what point in your life did you choose this career? 25

What is the longest document you ever had to write?..........26

Do you find email effective?...............................28

When is the right time to escalate an issue?.........................29

What is the riskiest decision you have ever made? 30

How do you deal with overseas coordination? 31

What is the worst job you ever had? 32

Have you ever had to work weekends? 33

Do you actually enjoy work?...34

Do you prefer to be a project manager or one of the team? ...35

What does project management mean to you? 36

Which one of your previous jobs was the most dynamic and why?..37

How do you approach an important assignment?.................38

How do you keep the big picture in mind when dealing with day-to-day issues?...39

How do you stay ahead of the competition? 40

Do you let the team know of higher-level issues pertaining to the company? 41

What are the challenges of dealing across departments or functions?...42

Tell me about a situation where you used your creativity?....44

Have you ever had to accept extra assistance in a project? 45

How can one be successful in this industry?..........................46

What motivates you in the work place? 47

What would your colleagues say about you? 48

Can you give an example of your leadership qualities? 49

Have you ever led a team? 50

What is the largest team you have led?.................................51

Have you ever spoken at conferences? 52

How adept at technology are you? 53

Are you a big picture or a detailed person? 54

How do you keep up with developments in the industry?....55

Why did your previous firm not live up to your expectations? 56

What are some of the structural changes you would make to this company? 57

Have you ever over engineered a solution beyond the obvious answer?..58

Give me an example of a time when you showed initiative in the work place?..59

CHAPTER 3: THE COMPANY AND THE ROLE IN QUESTION 61

Introduction 61

What is it about the company that attracts you here? 62

What do you know about the company? 63

Tell me something positive you have heard about the company? 64

Have you ever heard anything negative about this company? 65

What changes would you make to the company?................66

Do you think that your recent experience is relevant to this role? 67

What attracts you to the position?.....................................68

Why should I hire you over the other well-qualified candidates? 69

Do you think that you are qualified for the position? 70

Aren't you over qualified for this role? 71

Are you willing to start on a lesser role and we can re-assess later? 72

Why should I not hire you? 73

What happens if you don't get this role? 74

Your title would be different here – is that an issue? 75

If we made you an offer right now – would you accept? 76

How do you rate this interview? 77

Do you have questions for me? 78

CHAPTER 4: BEHAVIORAL QUESTIONS 81

Introduction 81

Have you ever fired anyone? 81

Describe a situation where you identified and mitigated a risk? 82

How do you deal with failure? 83

What happens if a person on your team is not pulling their weight? 84

How do you establish a rapport with clients or customers? ...85

How long does it take you to reach a decision? 86

How do you establish credibility with your team? 88

What is the best way to communicate with management? ...89

What happens when results are not up to your manager's
expectations? 90

Have you ever been unhappy with your own performance on a
project? 91

What kind of boss do you work best for? 92

Have you ever made decisions without having all the
information? 93

How do you deal with multi-tasking projects? 95

How do you react when you are passed over
for promotion? 96

Have you ever become angry at work? 97

Do you have any record of indiscipline? 98

What do you expect from a manager? 99

Why do you think you are a team player? 100

What happens when someone says no to you? 101

When did you have to pull out the stops and go above your
station? 102

What really irritates you in the work place?.......................103

Do you have difficulties working with some people and why?...104

What kind of hours do you like to keep? 105

What sort of pressure have you been under in the workplace? 106

How loyal are you? 106

What is the biggest mistake you have made to date in the workplace? 107

Have you ever had a dispute with a boss?...........................108

How do you deal with conflict? 109

Can you adapt to someone else's mode of work? 110

Have you ever been put on the spot?..................................111

How good are you at delegating?..112

Do you tend to aim too high? 113

Give an example of when you used good judgment............114

Have you ever managed to change someone's opinion?.......116

Have you ever changed your opinion? 117

What do you do if you fundamentally disagree with a
company policy?...118

Have you ever had a personal conflict with a colleague? 119

What do you do with confidential information?..................120

Have you ever had to adapt to a culturally different
environment? 121

What is the best way to react in a work crisis?....................122

How rigid do you stick to your goals? 124

What happens if you miss your goals? 125

Has your work ever been criticized by peers? 126

How do you deal with irate customers?...............................127

CHAPTER 5: SALARY EXPECTATION, RELOCATION AND RESIGNATION 129

Introduction 129

What are your salary expectations? 130

We can't pay you the kind of money you have been earning –
are you willing to take a pay cut?.......................................131

How come you have not earned as much as you should
have? 132

Are you expecting deferred compensation and/or share options from your previous firm to be paid? 132

Will you take shares or options in lieu of cash? 133

We cannot offer you a full comprehensive benefits package as we are too small –are you ok with that? 134

Are you leaving your current role for monetary reasons? 135

You have been with your company a long time – why switch now?...136

Will you find it difficult to leave your current company? ...137

You will be required to travel 25% of the time – is that an issue?..138

Are you will to relocate? 139

CHAPTER 6: YOUR EDUCATION 141

Introduction 141

What would you change about your college? 141

Are grades in reality an indication that you will do well in the workplace? 142

Why have you not considered a postgraduate degree? 144

Was that the school of your choice? 145

How do you rate the program there as against other schools? 146

What did you learn that is relevant? 147

How did your experience in school prepare you for business life? 148

What is your ideal job after graduation? 149

CHAPTER 7: CAREER BREAKS, OTHER PROSPECTS AND NUMBER OF PAST JOBS 151

Introduction 151

There is a long gap on your resume – what were you doing during that period? 152

Do you intend taking another break? 153

You have been out of work for a while –what have you being doing? 154

What criteria are you using to select companies to interview with? 155

You have been at many different companies in a short period of time? 156

Are you interviewing elsewhere?...157

What are your timescales? 158

CHAPTER 8: INTERESTS OUTSIDE THE WORKPLACE.. 159

Introduction 159

What are your outside interests?..159

What do you do for fun?..160

Do you speak any other languages? 161

Have you been inspired by any sporting figure? 162

Are you involved in charity or community work? 163

How can you channel external work activities into the
workplace? 164

What papers do you read?..166

CHAPTER 1: ALL ABOUT YOU

Introduction

The interviewer wants to know about you, what you are looking for and what motivates you. Expect some tough questions with respect to some of the choices and decisions you have made to date. You will be asked some general questions on what motivates you to work.

They will ask you certain questions to evaluate what you get out of working. What happens if you win the lottery – do you really still want to come to work and why?

You can expect some very standard interview questions relating to your strongest and weakest points.

The first few minutes of an interview will break the ice and it is vital to make a good impression that can set the tone for the rest of the interview.

What has been your biggest failure?

ANALYSIS: They are not necessary trying to get you to admit a past failure in the workplace but there will be an instance where a project or a person has failed to live up to expectations and you will have had some responsibility for this. Note that everyone has had some work situation that has gone wrong. The last thing the interviewer wants to hear is that you never have had any issues at all because this won't be credible. Your answer should admit to something having gone wrong but quickly demonstrate the positive that came out.

ANSWER1: There was a time when I failed to deliver goods to a client in time. He was irate and we nearly lost the account. I studied the full process leading up to these mistakes from what was promised to when it was promised. I learned that we did not fully understand the client's request and over promised on the solution. This is was a very valuable lesson and I have never repeated that failure.

ANSWER2: Senior management deemed a project that I was leading a failure at one time. For me, this was a lesson in how to communicate upwards. In fact the project had not failed from its intended goals but the senior management perception of what we were trying to achieve had become muddled because I hadn't communicated as frequent as I should have done. The situation was rectified and I improved my mode of communication.

ANSWER3: I just missed on getting into the course I wanted to at school and to me at the time this was the biggest failure of my life, disastrous even. However, the other course presented a similar challenge and in fact I was more determined to make it work for me. As I look back, I think that failure was in fact the best thing that ever happened to me.

∽

How would your best friend describe you?

ANALYSIS: Interviewers are not expecting to hear that your best friend thinks that you are the funniest person on earth and that no one can drink beer as well as you! They really want to know if you understand what your qualities are, how you interact, motivate and lead people and how trustworthy you are.

ANSWER1: My friendships are based on mutual respect. I have known my best friend since elementary school. We have been on many teams together. I have helped her with study, choosing school and with some life choices. I know that she trusts me and finds me loyal to a fault and therefore I believe that this is how she would describe me.

ANSWER2: My best friend would say the same about me as what I would say about him. He would say that I am one hundred percent loyal, hard working and a tough but fair competitor. We motivate each other to succeed and through some healthy competition, we have both really helped each other in our careers to date. I will always be there for my friend and he knows that.

ANSWER3: Life prepares you for work. The way you interact with people outside the office trickles into how you interact with people at the workplace. Trust, loyalty and mutual motivation are qualities that my friends expect of me and I would be very surprised if you were told otherwise.

ᕫᕬ

What is the toughest decision you have ever made?

ANALYSIS: You will have to make tough decisions especially if you are intending to move up the ladder. Interviewers will check your mindset and approach to decision making. They need to know that you are prepared to progress through the organization and are willing to make tough decisions. If they sense that you avoid such decisions, it will reflect negatively on you.

ANSWER1: The anticipation of a tough decision tends to be worse than the actual act. I had to cancel a project six months into it, much to the chagrin of the large project team. It was a pure business decision that made economic sense. I was careful in the way I broke the news to those involved so they knew it was not a reflection on their performance.

ANSWER2: Some of the toughest decisions are made outside the work place. In my final year at high school, I was given the opportunity to go to two great colleges, both of equal merit. I carefully weighed the pros and cons of each and made my final decision. It was a tough one but was made easier by my analysis. It was the right one in the long run.

ANSWER3: I had two star employees working for me but only one promotion slot due to the quota system. I knew if I chose one over the other, the other was likely to leave. I chose the one whom I felt was better in the long run for the business. The other one did leave. The promoted person excelled following the promotion and now runs the company!

∽

What is your best idea to date?

ANALYSIS: You may have many, so just choose one. They are not as interested in the idea itself but more the impact of the idea. What effect did the idea have on the product, team, company, school, industry or family? What role did you play once the idea was formulated?

ANSWER1: Our Company expanded very quickly and our product was flying off the shelves. We hired more new sales staff and the cost of training in terms of time and money was getting out of control. I commissioned a company intranet with internal social networking capabilities to share knowledge and experiences about our product. This cost effective approach has been a huge success and everyone has become dependent on it.

ANSWER2: Employees' morale was low mainly due to the effect of the recession on our product. We could not compensate as well as we used to in line with our competitors. I started a loyalty program where employees could nominate each other for a monthly gift. This program proved very popular and instilled a sense of pride to those who were rewarded.

ANSWER3: I think my best idea was to go to university. I had an offer to go to my uncle's business and there was some pressure on me to do so. It was my idea to further my education and it was the best idea ever. Aside from the academic experience, I built up a huge network of people that has proved very fruitful throughout my work life.

∾

What has been your biggest success?

ANALYSIS: The interviewers are not looking for a laundry list of your accomplishments to date. This question gives you the opportunity to demonstrate your broader management skills, team playing and functional knowledge.

ANSWER1: My biggest success has been to achieve a work life balance. I work hard and I play hard. On account of this, I have high energy levels to dedicate to my work. I have been consistently singled out as a high producer and I attribute this to the balance.

ANSWER2: My success is my team's success. We delivered a product, to a very demanding client a before the final deadline. The client was so impressed that we won ten more repeat orders and became their number one supplier. I was the project manager but I do attribute the success to great teamwork from the analysis to the delivery phase.

ANSWER3: I look at the successful completion of every task as the biggest success to date. Success does breed success and the more successful I am in one project, the bigger the challenge the next project will present. I think it is important in your career to keep building on everything you do.

༺༻

What would you have done differently if you started your work life again?

ANALYSIS: This is a reaction question with no real right answer. You do not want to come across as being embittered about the hand that life has dealt you to date. You need to remain positive and not portray yourself as a moaner or a potential gossiper!

ANSWER1: I had always wanted to be a programmer but for one reason or another, I never pursued this academically. A few years ago, I chose to change this and decided that I was going to become certified as a Java developer online. It took a lot of time but I got there. I guess it would have been a lot easier if I had studied this in the first instance but am very happy I had an opportunity to try other things first.

ANSWER2: I think we all look back from time to time and re-assess, that's quite natural. I believe that you should continue to live in the present and make the most of the opportunity in front of you. I would never have thought that I would have gone from working in a record shop to marketing at a multinational but that is what makes life exciting!

ANSWER3: I had to work extra hard in comparison to others on the graduate intake program as I had studied economics in school. My peers had degrees in business studies but I had mathematics. It was really easy for peers to grasp all the basics required for the job. At that time, I did wish that I had done something else in school but the mathematics came in useful later. I don't think there is too much point looking back as life is an accumulation of valuable experiences.

∽

What are the most important rewards you expect gain from your career?

ANALYSIS: Rewards do not need to be monetary. Interviewers will want to hear that satisfaction and fulfillment will play a large part in the rewards you expect. They are trying to see what motivates you and how that plays into your long term plans for yourself and this role.

ANSWER1: Being challenged and constantly learning are rewards for me. I believe that if you are highly motivated, then financial and promotional rewards will follow suit. I will not go somewhere for extra dollars if I know that the role is not going to be challenging.

ANSWER2: I really get a kick out of customer or client satisfaction. A simple thank you from a customer is a huge reward for me. It is an acknowledgment that you and your staff have accomplished a defined goal and have secured yet another satisfied customer.

ANSWER3: When I look down the ranks of an organization and see people who I have mentored as junior staff now progressing through the organization, I feel very proud. It is very rewarding to encourage and mould people in a shared vision that will reap success for them and the company.

∾

Sell me your shoes in 1 minute.

ANALYSIS: They are checking both your ability to think on your feet and also how succinctly you can get your point across. You will meet many busy people whom you have about 1 minute to impress or get your point across throughout your career.

ANSWER1: These shoes are unique. They were purchased in a market in Istanbul after a vigorous bartering session. I swore to myself that I would never sell them. However, I do feel comfortable selling to them to you, as I know you would take care of them. Let's just say one hundred dollars and we are done.

ANSWER2: You have asked if these shoes are for sale. They are pure leather and have hardly ever been worn. I need to ensure that they will be taken care of and I believe that you are the right person to have them. I will give you a thirty percent discount for a cash only purchase.

ANSWER3: These shoes are priceless and are not for sale. I am constantly approached by people for them and have been offered some ridiculous sums of money for them. I think people are attracted to the individualistic style and shape. I have seen you gaze at them intently. Why don't you let me know a price and maybe we can work something out.

୧୬

If you won the lottery tomorrow would you still work?

ANALYSIS: What are you working for? Is it simply money or do you actually enjoy it? What motivates you? What if you really did not have to work for monetary reasons – would you still bother? Interviewers really want to know how serious your ambitions are and commitment to them will be.

ANSWER1: I need to be constantly challenged. Winning the lottery, while nice from a financial point of view, would not mean that I intend to spend the rest of my life as a person of leisure. I absolutely intend to continue to work and it is challenging roles like this one that interest me.

ANSWER2: As far as I am concerned, the day you stop learning is the day you die. This role offers the opportunity to constantly learn, develop and grow my career. Even if I won the lottery, this sentiment would not change one bit.

ANSWER3: I have read that numerous stories of people having their lives ruined by winning the lottery. For me coming to work is not simply about money or amassing wealth in order to retire early. We all need a growth structure in our life and an opportunity like this provides such structure. No, I will definitely be working for as long as I can.

∽

What is the ideal role for you?

ANALYSIS: They want to know that you are the person the company is looking for to fill this role. You need to impress on them that you fully understand the role and are willing to evolve it within the ethos of the company. You should give both short term and long-term views.

ANSWER1: The ideal role for me is one that not only uses my experience to date but also allows me to grow in the future. I am looking for my next big move, my next eight to ten years and therefore the next move is huge for me. I understand that this role and company will allow me to grow. I expect to be in senior management running a division in this company within ten years.

ANSWER2: I always look to the long term; this role seems to have all the qualities to allow me to progress through your company in the longer term. My short-term aim is to learn as much about the product and its developments as I can. Then I want to build a team to take on the competitors.

ANSWER3: I am risk taker and as is evident from my resume have tried a few different paths. This role also presents risks but it is obviously very entrepreneurial to its core. I have never shunned a challenge and the opportunity to work with you and help this company evolve into some huge is very appealing to me. The first thing I would like to do is get the company's name branded and then I would embark on an aggressive marketing campaign. This is what I am good at!

◌

What are your three strongest points?

ANALYSIS: Your strong points should be both work related and relevant to the role. You should zone in on your ability to work with others. You are a good listener and take responsibility for your actions. Interviewers are looking for an all-rounder, not just someone to slot in for a few months.

ANSWER1: My strong points are problem identification, analysis and solving. I have a very strong track record of being able to break a goal or a problem down into components, analyze what needs to done and propose a logical strategy for a solution with realistic timelines. In many cases, I lead the execution of the strategy myself.

ANSWER2: I have great experience in building a team from scratch, optimizing productivity from each of the team members whilst keeping the overall goals in mind and driving the team to complete the tasks in a timely manner. This triplicate of skills has been very successful over and over again.

ANSWER3: My career has flourished over the past few years and I attribute this to perfecting three goals. Firstly, I really learned how to listen to peers and value their opinions. Secondly,

I have become more adept at managing client's expectations and thirdly, I have managed to create a work-life balance that makes me more productive.

∽

What are your weakest points?

ANALYSIS: An interview favorite. You need to demonstrate that in the past you have identified a weakness but have worked hard to deal with it and have overcome it now. They are more interested in your ability to grow and mature than a laundry list of weakness and insecurities that will reflect very negatively on you.

ANSWER1: I found public speaking to be an issue. I felt that it was a weak point in my career arsenal. I used to dread for days anytime I had to make a presentation. I believe we all have weak points and that is normal but you have to work on them. I spent more and more time practicing my presentations at home and soon this weakness was overcome. I now regularly give presentations and speak at conferences.

ANSWER2: I used to try to please too hard. A customer would set a very aggressive and unrealistic deadline and I would agree to it. This used to drive my team crazy. Over the years, I have worked hard to develop negotiation skills and now my customers are set realistic and achievable deadlines.

ANSWER3: My time management skills were really bad when I started work. I used to work sixteen hours a day but not all of it could be charged and also I was having no life outside the office. I took an online course at the weekends and realized what I was doing wrong. I managed to turn my weak point around and today have a much more productive life inside and outside the office.

∾

What makes you get out of bed in the morning?

ANALYSIS: It may the alarm clock or the kids, but that is not what they are asking. This is an opportunity for you again to demonstrate how motivated you are and that you have a "seize the day" mentality. They will see that such energy will convert well in the work place.

ANSWER1: I really enjoy the fresh challenge that every new day brings. This is why a role like this is so appealing to me as it presents various tasks and challenges that will keep both the team and me active throughout the day.

ANSWER2: Everyday brings an element of the unknown. Who really knows what happens in both your work and personal life today. This is what makes living so worthwhile.

ANSWER3: I like to set myself goals for each day. Some may be trivial like doing laundry but all contribute to a sense of accomplishment. Similarly, I plan my work day in my head in the morning setting myself achievable goals for that day with the end objective getting closer each day.

⁓

How do you rate your communication skills?

ANALYSIS: Written and oral communication skills are crucial in the workplace. They are looking for some concrete examples from your experiences to date (be they in or outside the workplace). They need to know that you understand the importance of such a skill set.

ANSWER1: I have spoken at many conferences as part of my last role. I made it look easy but only because I was very well prepared. The key to good communication is preparation. The more you understand and have researched a topic, the better you can communicate. I always prepare myself in advance of meetings with clients and colleagues.

ANSWER2: I have worked very hard on my communication skills over the years to the extent that I do rank them very highly. I bundle communication as being a good listener, the ability to summarize issues concisely in both verbal and written format and the delivery of key points in varying detail to different layers of management. At every team meeting, I am the one to review the topics from the last time and to set the agenda.

ANSWER3: I do not think it is possible to survive in any form of business without strong communication skills. You do not need to be a university debating champion but everyone needs the basics whether dealing with colleagues or clients. I am able to engage with clients, colleagues and senior managers on account of my strong skills. Clients constantly ask for me when they call the office, as they know I can concisely give them the information they need.

෮

What are your main goals?

ANALYSIS: They are expecting that your main goals will be in tune with the role and the company's vision. Anything different will be construed as a real lack of interest or commitment to the company. You should have clear and concise goals in mind.

ANSWER1: I am ambitious for both my employers and myself. I have a very practical view of the world and am very positive. I always want to remain positive and focused inside and outside the workplace. With these goals, I can achieve anything I put my mind to. I have followed your company's recent progress and I believe that with some practical changes to your production process, the company could move to number one in this sector.

ANSWER2: I want to be in senior management within three years. I believe that this is a very attainable goal based on my achievements to date and the skills I have accumulated. I believe that this company and role has the support structure for such a goal and I would work hard to attain it.

ANSWER3: My goals are simple: I want to be constantly challenged and keep learning over my career. This is really important to me and I believe that the rewards will follow suit.

Learning can be in many forms such as new role, new people, new regulation, new clients and new problems! One of the main reasons I am interviewing here as I see this role as a challenge with the right rewards to satisfy my ambitions.

৩৯

Do you consider yourself lucky?

ANALYSIS: This is to check your positivity. You make own your luck and therefore they expect to hear that yes you are lucky but your luck has been due to hard work and ethic.

ANSWER1: I have never won the lottery but I do absolutely feel lucky! I am lucky that I had the opportunity to get an education, have career success and now have the opportunity to look to further my career prospects. I believe in life that you make your own luck to a large extent through hard work.

ANSWER2: I have worked really hard to get where I am and am very appreciative of that. On relative terms, I am lucky as there are many worse off in the world. Lucky or not, my determination to learn and succeed has never waned one bit.

ANSWER3: If you had asked me a few years ago, I certainly would not have considered myself lucky at all. I was involved in a nasty car crash that pretty much rendered me immobile for a number of months. After a brief period of feeling sorry for myself, I used the time to learn how to develop in C sharp. It was a great use of my time and in fact I am lucky I took a positive approach to my healing.

❧

Do you have a personal mission statement?

ANALYSIS: Your personal mission statement should be in sync with the role that you are applying for. If you are way off base, it will be confusing to the interviewer. Your statement should also contain some general statement about life-work balance.

ANSWER1: My mission statement is to work hard and live life to the full. I believe that if you remain challenged, focused and keep on learning, you will reap the benefits that will allow you and your family live a more fruitful life. A role like the one on offer would allow me to pursue my mission.

ANSWER2: I think that it is possible to have a statement of some sort and maybe that is a good thing. However, it is best to break the statement into short-term goals as life and work evolve and you need to adapt with it. The underlying theme should be to stay positive in and outside the work place. My approach to work is similar as I break my long-term goals into mini attainable goals.

ANSWER3: I don't have a personal mission statement, as I am a firm advocate of the team model. If I had to have a mission statement in terms of approach to work, then I would expect my team to have the same statement. I have come across many people with their own agenda and they are the ones who tend not to be team players.

∽

What is your measure of success?

ANALYSIS: You will need to have some measure of success within the workplace. Interviewers need to know that you are capable of setting a goal and then measuring yourself against how well you reach it. Success in definition can vary from hiring the right team to launching a product in a timely manner.

ANSWER1: At the outset of any project, I set myself goals and I measure myself against them. These goals include timelines, expected quality of work and mode of delivery for the team. Being successful also includes the ability to be flexible to redefine goals if the parameters of the project change during its lifecycle.

ANSWER2: You are as successful as the people around you. Therefore a huge measure of success is to hire and retain quality staff around you. You should always try to hire people who are better than you and who are willing to work in the team environment.

ANSWER3: I like to help and encourage junior members of staff. I believe that this is the key to the success of the company's strategy. The next generation must share both the ambition and the vision of the company. I created a mentoring program where senior employees spend two hours a month motivating and helping individual employees.

∾

Where do you see yourself in a number of years?

ANALYSIS: Very much a crowd favorite and a very misunderstood question. This is a true test of your ambition and commitment to the company. In addition, interviewers are also testing how realistic your expectations are. Are you interviewing for one role but really just want to get your foot in the door to switch to another department at the first opportunity? Do you really see a career path in area you are interviewing in or are you intending to get experience and then leave the company? Recruiting is expensive and taken very seriously. They need to be convinced that you have really thought this through and are committed to the company.

ANSWER1: I fully understand this role and your company's future plans. These are both fully in sync with my own ambitions. I expect that the primary focus for a number of years will be this role and the associated product line. I would then like to take on a senior position similar to yours where I would be in charge of leading a number of divisions for the company.

ANSWER2: As this is my first role out of school, I know that I have a steep learning curve ahead of me. For the next few years, I intend to learn as much as I possibly can about the company, the industry and this opportunity. I believe that the early part in anyone's career is a vital stepping-stone to management. The career structure here will help me succeed into middle and then senior management.

ANSWER3: I have researched this profession by reading as much as I can and even work shadowing on occasion. I am lucky in that I know what I want to do now and in the future. This interview process has consolidated that view for me. I expect to gain the right professional qualifications and move up the ladder as quickly as I can at this company.

ᕦᕤ

How strong are your analytical skills?

ANALYSIS: Don't underestimate the analytical skills you have. You don't have to have a doctorate from Harvard to demonstrate analytical ability. They will want to know how you identified an issue, worked out a solution and implemented it. This is a key skill in the work arena.

ANSWER1: I have an academic background in engineering and one of the tenets of that course was the ability to analyze a problem in minute detail and work out a solution in logical steps. I don't use my engineering in practical terms at my current role but the analytical skills I learned are very valuable in dealing with all sorts of problems and decisions I am faced with.

ANSWER2: I have no formal analytical training. I studied history at school. However, it became apparent that analytical skills are very much core to the work place. I have read many practical case studies on how to approach problem solving in the work place and applied what I learned to great effect. Now, I am on a par with anyone who has mathematics or engineering degrees in terms of work related analytical skills such as use of spreadsheets and practical problem solving.

ANSWER3: I do have real world experience in problem assessment. I am consistently nominated to manage many of the new processes and issues we come across. My ability to understand a problem, break it down and work out a solution within a team environment has helped me climb the ladder quickly over the last few years.

∽

Have you done your best work yet?

ANALYSIS: They expect to hear that your work is still evolving and that you expect your best work is still to come. Naturally the work you have performed to date has been of quality but now you have more experience as you look for the next role.

ANSWER1: I believe that throughout your career, you continue to evolve both as a person and as a colleague. I learn from every piece of work I do. I review every role that I had and ensure that I learn what I did right and wrong. I find that with each new piece of work I do, I get better and better.

ANSWER2: I have achieved much success to date and on occasion, bosses and senior management have indicated that that was my best work to date. But I believe that there is much more to do and with every challenge, I can better my work again.

ANSWER3: I am not convinced that anyone can claim to have done his or her best work. I am just about to enter the work force and I believe that I have fifty years of best work ahead of me. For me, my best work is when I feel fully satisfied that I can learn no more and there are no more problems for me to solve. I know that this is unrealistic so therefore my best work is yet to come.

CHAPTER 2: YOUR CAREER TO DATE

Introduction

Interview questions that specifically deal with your career are some of the toughest.

They will delve into your leadership skills, your ability to be a team member and your communications skills.

Also, expect questions on your industry and regulation experience.

You will need examples of initiative, creativity and how you have implemented change to date.

༄

At what point in your life did you choose this career?

ANALYSIS: There is no right answer to this question but they want to see how committed you are to this role, the industry and your goals. It is very unlikely (outside defined professions such as doctor, dentist, and soldier) that you have been thinking about this industry since you were six years of age. You could have stumbled into this area and that is perfectly acceptable.

ANSWER1: When I was in high school, I thought that I wanted to be a doctor. However, when I bought my first computer, I got addicted to the creative process. The evolution in this area over the past ten years has been mind blowing. I have probably programmed every day of my life since then.

ANSWER2: I started selling lemonade at the age of seven outside my own home. It was my first business venture and I unwittingly learned about supply, demand and margin. I parlayed the dollars earned into buying and selling comic books. I have continued this entrepreneurial activity throughout my life and that is why I love sales roles like the position open here.

ANSWER3: My first job was accountancy. I worked, studied and subsequently passed the exams. I found the discipline of this study challenging when my ex college friends were having fun but it was worth it. As my career evolves, I have gravitated towards business development but I don't underestimate the importance of my accounting skills in this new career path.

What is the longest document you ever had to write?

ANALYSIS: Document writing is going to be necessary at some stage. Documents can be reports, management summaries, competitor analysis, functional specifications etc. They are more interested in your approach to writing documents rather than the actual length of the document. How well was the document received? Were there any revisions?

ANSWER1: Clear communication is a must in the work place. Earlier in my career, I was a business analyst and was the interface between the business and technology departments. I had to clearly define the requirements in functional specification documents that could range from fifty to two hundred pages. These had to be written in such a way that an offshore IT resource would know exactly what to code. My success with communication was integral to my promotion to project manager.

ANSWER2: I have had to write many report summaries for senior management. In general these reports are quite short and these can be trickier than longer ones. A summary report needs to condense the theme and the message from the long report onto one page. The ability to communicate information concisely on paper is vital in the workplace and I have honed that skill over the years.

ANSWER3: To date, my final year thesis has been the longest document I have ever written. I was studying the movement of plate tectonics under the world's oceans. The final document was a culmination of long hours of research and even longer hours of drafting and re-drafting. I really learned to appreciate the value of clearly written and flowing documents with correct grammar and construction. This will be very useful to me in the workplace.

∾

Do you find email effective?

ANALYSIS: Email is a very valuable tool and has proved to be a very effective mode of communication but it should not be the only mode. Some people have a tendency to hide behind email and never engage in open dialog or confrontation. They want to know that you are able to balance different modes of communication.

ANSWER1: Email has become a global phenomenon over the past 15 years. It is hard to understand what we did before email in some cases. I do think it is an effective mode of communication especially in companies with many offices scattered regionally and globally. Naturally, one should also make an effort to meet and talk with colleagues and clients as well.

ANSWER2: It is important to balance the use of email against the traditional modes of communication. There can be a tendency to hide behind email especially in times of conflict. People still need to be able to air their thoughts and issues face to face. Email is great but should not be the only mode of communication.

ANSWER3: Email is certainly cost effective and has made the world a smaller place. A side effect of the email revolution is that client interaction and expectation management has become more difficult. People now expect real-time responses, which is not always realistic. Email should be a tool in your business arsenal but should not be the dominant strategy execution tool.

∽

When is the right time to escalate an issue?

ANALYSIS: They want to know that you will take control and responsibility yourself. Escalating every issue will annoy your team and your management will begin to think that you are incapable.

ANSWER1: I think it is important to exhaust all avenues before escalating an issue. Negotiation and conflict management skills are vital for anyone who wants to progress in one's career. I found that there was always a resolution to be found by open dialog. A person in another department who was vital to our production process was constantly unresponsive to our requests for data. People in my team wanted me to just go to his boss. Instead, I asked him to go for a coffee and explained how vital he was to our process. Once he understood, he was never a bottleneck again.

ANSWER2: Some people have the tendency to escalate an issue at every available opportunity. I believe that by overusing this tactic you bring a lack of credibility to your own role. In addition, the person whom you escalate to, will begin to doubt your effectiveness. Therefore I limit the times I escalate.

ANSWER3: Sometimes if time is of critical importance or if someone is absolutely becoming a bottleneck on the critical path of a project, then you need to escalate for the sake of progression of the project. If you feel that you have to keep doing this on account of one person, then you need take action with this person.

∾

What is the riskiest decision you have ever made?

ANALYSIS: There is maverick risk and measured risk. They want to know that you are not going to put a company's reputation or business at risk with a rash decision. However, they will be expecting to hear about measured risks you have taken, why you took those decisions, what the outcome was and what you learned.

ANSWER1: I decided to start the branding of a new product before it entered its first test cycle. Some of my colleagues felt that this was a bit too risky. I trusted my team; they were confident and we wanted first mover advantage. My team and I were very experienced and felt that it was a measured risk. The branding department did a great job and we were first to market with the product.

ANSWER2: When I was fifteen, I really thought that I wanted to be a writer so I studied English Literature, History and Arts in school. However about eighteen months later, I developed a huge interest in Engineering. I decided to apply to a school to study engineering. It was risky in the sense that I did have to work three times as hard as my peers to catch up but it paid off.

ANSWER3: When I was at a start-up, I promised a number of items to our seed capital investors. This could have been construed as aggressive and risky in terms of over promise. However, I know my own ability and capacity to work as many hours as I have to, to make things happen. The investors were pleased. You have to trust yourself also.

෴

How do you deal with overseas coordination?

ANALYSIS: Overseas coordination can be really tricky. You have to reach out to people who speak different languages, are stationed in different time zones and have different more localized priorities. In many cases, you will not know or have never met the people. You will need an arsenal of negotiation and diplomatic skills to properly coordinate business like this.

ANSWER1: My previous role was to lead a team with people based in India, Hong Kong, London and Boston. Budgets were tight so there was absolutely no scope for travelling. I used all the communication available to me such as email, web video and shared web sites for status updates. I appointed one person in each region to be responsible for running the segment in that region. I ensured that all communication channels remained open.

ANSWER2: My suppliers were based in Thailand and China. They had come well recommended from old colleagues. I like to build relationships so I travelled to both countries, shook hands, and had some drinks and dinner to cement the relationship. Once back, I ensured that I kept the relationship strong through email, web tracking, follow-up phone calls and via video conference calls. I still travel once a year to ensure that the supplier knows that our relationship is important.

ANSWER3: I was the administrator for the tennis team in school. We invited teams from London, Japan and Spain to come play against us in a biennial competition. I had to arrange the tournament and the logistics. I made great use of email and social networking sites to help with the coordination and it worked perfectly. The world has become a smaller place and there are many tools available to us today to help with cross-global coordination.

೧௨

What is the worst job you ever had?

ANALYSIS: Having a bad job does not have to be a bad experience. The "worst" could be a paper round or working as a "tea lady". You learn something in every job. You learn about people and interactions that will serve you later in your working career. They will be interested to hear about the experiences you have drawn.

ANSWER1: When I was in college, I had a part time job at a video production plant. My role was simply to stack videos into boxes and I was paid less than minimum wage for the pleasure of doing so. That job really spurred me on to study harder and make the grades that helped me to get me to where I am in my career now.

ANSWER2: In my last company, we unfortunately filed for bankruptcy through chapter 11 and the company had to be wound down in an orderly fashion. My role was to oversee the wind down and therefore I had to lay off four hundred people over a two month period. I learned the tough side of business during that period but conducted myself in a professional manner and did what needed to be done.

ANSWER3: I don't believe it is possible to have a bad job. Even if you dislike your job at a certain time, you are still learning valuable skills either directly or through osmosis. Every challenge or even every boring moment should spur you to reach the next level. You got to keep on learning to succeed and this has been my approach.

✎

Have you ever had to work weekends?

ANALYSIS: They want to see how flexible you are. This is to test your commitment to completing a task. Sometimes (actually most times) deadlines are very aggressive and you will be stretched to reach them. They are checking your appetite to work under that kind of pressure.

ANSWER1: Yes, I have and that has not been an issue for me. There are times when deadlines have to be met. Clients are becoming increasingly demanding and the competition in this area is fierce. If an order or a project has to be met, then of course, I will put in the extra hours.

ANSWER2: Working weekends these days is more common than in the past. Most people can log into their company networks via their home computer and many have portable devices such as PDAs and the likes. I find that sometimes I can clear my workload during a quiet period at the weekend.

ANSWER3: I have never had to work weekends but have no problem in doing so if necessary. I believe that everyone should have a flexible approach to work. Being more flexible helps meet deadlines and I want you know that you can rely on me to go that extra mile to get things done.

∽

Do you actually enjoy work?

ANALYSIS: They do not want to hire someone who is going to be miserable and just keep one eye on the clock waiting for the day to end. Likewise, it won't be very credible if you enjoy work more than a night out with your friends. The more you enjoy your work, the more productive you will be and you also need to have a work-life balance.

ANSWER1: In fact I do! I really like the challenges and the interaction with colleagues during the day. Many companies and especially yours have worked hard to make the work experience better for everyone. I think that people who claim to hate their work are very unlucky and probably very unproductive.

ANSWER2: A company's greatest asset is its employees. The happier the employees are, the more productive they and the company will be. Naturally work is not a holiday camp, but it is important to strike a balance between pressure and enjoyment. I have always been happy at my work place.

ANSWER3: I really want to enjoy my work. It is really important to me as I feel I am more productive when happy. The reason that I am looking for a new role is because of the unique opportunity you are offering and the global nature of the role. My current employers cannot offer me such an opportunity.

ᏋᏊ

Do you prefer to be a project manager or one of the team?

ANALYSIS: There will times when you will be the leader and others when you will be one of the team. You need to demonstrate to the interviewers that you are not a prima Dona who always needs to be in charge. Likewise, you need to convince them that you are willing to step up to lead when required.

ANSWER1: I relish responsibility and therefore I always put my hand up to be project manager. I have a very strong track record of being a project manager and I believe that my ability to analyze a task, break it down into milestones and then gather the right team mix has really helped me to be successful.

ANSWER2: In reality, the way I work, it is possible to be both. I work on a large number of projects at any one time, some I manage and others I am a team member. The benefit of being a team member on some projects means I learn more tips from the project managers on those projects.

ANSWER3: I am quite junior in terms of rank at my company and the senior ranks tend to be given the project manager roles. However, I believe that I am ready to be a project manager and this is one of the reasons I am looking to leave. I believe that if someone is strong enough to lead, then they should be given that opportunity. I know that your company is open to this.

༄

What does project management mean to you?

ANALYSIS: The answer must include actually getting the project done in a timely manner. They are looking for your approach to analyzing the task, breaking it down into reachable milestones, identifying a team and producing the project plan to be ratified by senior management.

ANSWER1: Project management is the mode by which you get a job done. You can be a team of five or five hundred but the process is similar. You must define the problem, analyze it, form a strategy to get to the solution and create a team with measurable tasks to execute the strategy.

ANSWER2: Responsibility is key for project managers. They will be held accountable and therefore must have very clear and achievable goals set. Constant communication with the sponsor or client is key to the success of the project. The worst time to disengage a client is when things are going wrong.

ANSWER3: My approach to project management is to think of myself as the client and then I can better understand what should be expected from the product or solution. I work backwards from there and set definable and iterative deliverables to show progress along the way. I encourage open dialog with all team members so any issues are dealt with swiftly.

~⦿~

Which one of your previous jobs was the most dynamic and why?

ANALYSIS: They want to see what you deem dynamic or not and they will map this to the role on offer. If you give the impression that your last role was boring beyond belief and it is similar to this role, then they will question your motivation and reasons for applying for this job.

ANSWER1: I really enjoyed the entrepreneurial role during my time at Company ABC. The chance to build a business from the inception of an idea was very challenging but very rewarding. I touched all areas of the business from product creation to marketing. I see a lot of similarities to this role and that is why I applied.

ANSWER2: I love working in this industry and have been doing so for 14 years now. The people and the culture create a very stimulating environment. The pace of change is sometimes hard to keep up with but that is what makes it exciting. I can't see myself working outside the industry so in reality all my previous roles have been dynamic.

ANSWER3: I would not have stayed too long in any role if it was not dynamic and challenging but if I had to single out one, it would be the time spent as an analyst. In this role, you had to be a self-starter, reach out to clients on a regular basis and communicate to senior management through reports and status meetings. I was really kept on my toes and thoroughly enjoyed it.

ᘖ

How do you approach an important assignment?

ANALYSIS: In theory, every assignment is important and should be treated as such. They expect that you will be able to differentiate and prioritize among the numerous tasks you have at any one time. At the very least, you should know who is able to prioritize tasks for you. You need to indicate that you don't just jump feet first into an assignment and you have some methodical way of approaching each task.

ANSWER1: In reality, every assignment is important and I treat them all as so. Understanding the requirements is the most important initial step. You should not be afraid to ask all the questions you need. Not all the facts will be known but you can definitely start preparing your solution and plans.

ANSWER2: I like to have a kickoff meeting with all the interested parties. The purpose is to share ideas, understand what needs to be done, brainstorm a solution, allocate tasks and put names to faces. Different assignments can mean different people who may never have worked together before. It is important to build a team spirit and responsibility from the outset.

ANSWER3: I like to ensure that the project is mandated and budgeted properly. I have seen some excitement created around projects that have no budget. Once the budget is secured, I research the requirements, determine the skill sets required and assemble the best team available while accounting for competing priorities.

෴

How do you keep the big picture in mind when dealing with day-to-day issues?

ANALYSIS: All your day-to-day tasks and issues should be keeping the big picture common goal in mind. They will expect you to know the big picture, where to get the information and how to communicate with your team. Understanding priority and goals is key to the success of the company.

ANSWER1: You would have to question the motivation of someone who doesn't know the big picture of the firm. Either they are just coming to work on a daily basis just to collect a check with no ambition of moving upwards or their senior management has failed to inform them. Neither is a good scenario, I always wanted to know where the company is going and where my colleagues and I fit in. This really motivates me.

ANSWER2: I don't believe that you can effectively conduct your day-to-day duties unless you really understand the importance of them to the organization. Any organization is like a big production factory machine. Every department is a cog in the wheel. Senior management needs all employees to know how important their function is to the production.

ANSWER3: I was in charge of a charity drive to raise one hundred thousand dollars for an inner city housing project. There were fifteen people on the team all with different roles, some on the phones, others seeking corporate sponsorship and others developing an online campaign. I ensured that everyone regardless of position came to see firsthand the needs we were trying to address and what we were aiming for. I think that everyone needs to have knowledge of the big picture at all times where possible.

How do you stay ahead of the competition?

ANALYSIS: Every business has a competitor and in most cases you will have many. You will need to know your market place and the strength and weaknesses of your competitors. Your clients will know who your competitors are and they will expect you to also. They will want to know how you keep a check on the competition.

ANSWER1: Knowing your competitors is vital, whether you are an established business or a startup. My team constantly reviews company websites, annual reports and any press releases for hidden messages. We have four direct competitors selling the same or similar products. We keep a close eye on their price points, discounts, distribution channels and estimate what inventory they may have. These factors do contribute to our pricing as well.

ANSWER2: In this high volume/low margin sector, competition is tight. You have to stay ahead and fend off your competition. Employees are the biggest asset. You need to do your best to keep your employees motivated, their compensation competitive and ensure they feel that they have career growth. If you lose many employees, you will put your business at risk and empower your competitors.

ANSWER3: When I was in school, I wanted to earn some extra money by setting up an on-campus laundry service. I would hire some people to collect, wash and drop the laundry back same day. There were five launderettes within a three mile radius, each offered delivery but none collection. As part of my competitive analysis I researched their prices per pound, the proximity to campus, the cutoff for delivery times and polled their customers to see how happy people were. I improved the client experience in every category. You always need to know what your competitors are doing.

Do you let the team know of higher-level issues pertaining to the company?

ANALYSIS: As you move up the ladder in an organization, you will become more privy to company strategy, results and future plans. There is a balancing act between telling your team everything so they completely trust you, telling them only what you are allowed to or telling them nothing at all. You can only tell what you are allowed and you should never exclude them especially if other managers have given information out.

ANSWER1: I like to keep my team as informed as I possibly can. This helps build up trust and a healthy open relationship. Naturally, there will be some items that I cannot discuss with everyone but if you have a good relationship, the team will understand that also.

ANSWER2: Senior management items such as legal issues or potential redundancies are not things that you can or should discuss with more junior staff. However, everyone needs to have a sense of ownership in the company and not just by owning shares or options. It is very motivational for everyone to feel a part of the company.

ANSWER3: My last role was quite junior and I didn't have a team so I wasn't privy to all the information or the issues the company was going through. We used to hear things from people outside the firm and they seemed to know more than we did. I think it is very important for senior management to be as inclusive as possible.

◌

What are the challenges of dealing across departments or functions?

ANALYSIS: Even if you are all under the umbrella of one company, there is always some latent internal competition among different departments. The reason for this is that each department has its own implied hierarchy, sub culture, priorities and in some cases budget. Obtaining interdepartmental assistance can be a challenge and the interviewer expects that you are aware of the issues and have ways to address them to get the job done.

ANSWER1: Although every department has the bigger picture in focus and the company strategy in mind, they still have their own priorities. It can be difficult to get cooperation without a higher mandate sometimes. I believe that it is important to build up your own network across a company. This can be comprised of people whom I met at orientation, training course, social-events or through colleagues. This is a great way to help each other at the grassroots levels.

ANSWER2: If a mandate has been given to all departments to cooperate on a central initiative, then you need each department to appoint a key person for the project. For example, if a bank wanted to implement a new customer system, you would need a key person from IT, operations, legal, compliance, networks and marketing to assist. A project manager would coordinate among all these key people to implement the system.

ANSWER3: My last Company was a startup so we didn't have departments. We were all one big department! However we did all have our functions and on occasion over exuberance did cause some to pull in a different directions. I learned that all functions and departments should be mandated to work together under the direction of senior management.

∽

Tell me about a situation where you used your creativity?

ANALYSIS: You do not have to be a full time artist to be creative. In the workplace, creativity is required in many situations. Product creation, solution analysis, conflict resolution, client interaction and team management are examples. Have some examples of situations where you have been creative and that have had an impact on a problem and its solution.

ANSWER1: I took over the role of editor of the college newspaper. I immediately noticed that the paper had pretty much used up its small grant. We were on the verge of closing down. I created an online raffle where the prize was a full-page profile and interview with the winner. With the raffle money and the advertisement space sold, we secured enough financing to survive.

ANSWER2: There was much duplicity in our production processes. Many of the stages were manual and inefficient. I reviewed the processes fully front to back and created a solution that automated much of the product lifecycle. This saved us millions in production costs.

ANSWER3: Our clients send us a lot of email with a lot of useful information that could be used by other people in the group. Our email system automatically deletes our mails after thirty days. I commissioned a website to be built where the emails were categorized and forwarded on automatically. Now everyone in the group can retrieve the information easily.

༑

Have you ever had to accept extra assistance in a project?

ANALYSIS: Even the best intended projects or product launches do not always go according to plan. Sometimes it is necessary to ask for more help. Some people are afraid to do this for reasons of pride or fear of failure but ultimately they have to or the project will suffer. The interviewers want to understand what you would do in this situation.

ANSWER1: I have asked for and am not afraid to ask for more resources on a project if I need them. Scope changes, clients' shifting parameters and external factors can influence change at any time. If you put forward a good case for the extra resources showing clearly the extra benefits, then the assistance is justified.

ANSWER2: Many people early in their careers are afraid to put their hand up for extra help. This can lead to stress, lack of quality output or a realization that you maybe in the wrong role. It takes a certain level of career maturity to balance when to ask for help and justify why you need it. I have had to do this on occasion.

ANSWER3: I worked in a startup where it was all hands on deck. We could have all done with more help but in reality there was none to be had by way of resource. I approached it in a different way by cutting out some of the existing tasks. It really taught me how to focus on priorities. I have developed that skill over time so tend not to ask for help unless critical.

ᘒ

How can one be successful in this industry?

ANALYSIS: There are various ways to be successful in any industry. Your answer can be generic to suit many industries. Have a few points prepared that center around the qualities that make senior managers standout such as leadership, teamwork, communication, analytical and strategic thinking.

ANSWER1: I believe the more rounded you are as a person, the better chance you have to succeed in this and in any industry. Success is a multi-dimensional composition of leadership, academic prowess, motivation, team playing and communication. There may be some luck involved but you really make your own in this world.

ANSWER2: You need to be on top of the factors that drive your industry. This includes product knowledge, competitor awareness, market place and regulation. This knowledge needs to be channeled into management skills such as vision, team leadership, analysis and communication.

ANSWER3: Hard work. Without hard work, you will depend on luck and that is not a good approach. The harder you work, the more you learn. If you stop learning, you will become stale and will not progress. You will not impress or lead your colleagues and they will move ahead of you. For me, it's all about hard work.

෬

What motivates you in the work place?

ANALYSIS: They are looking for all rounder. They will expect that you are conscious of reaching your defined goals and also you have the firm's objectives at heart. This includes assisting with employee mentoring, recruiting, team leadership, customer service and constant self-improvement.

ANSWER1: I love teamwork and really get a buzz out of completing tasks and deliverables. Some are more stressful than others but the sense of accomplishment spurs me on to look forward to the next challenge. I enjoy working in an environment that allows you to continuously evolve.

ANSWER2: For me boredom at work is the worst form of stress. I am constantly looking for ways to improve my knowledge and experience in the workplace. I look at the accomplished leaders inside and outside firm for motivation. I feel the more skills you acquire; the more motivated you will be to aspire to higher goals.

ANSWER3: Customer satisfaction is a huge motivating factor for my team and me. There is something very tangible about delivery to customers. Seeing something from inception, design, creation, production and delivery to the client is very gratifying and really spurs me on

∽

What would your colleagues say about you?

ANALYSIS: They are not expecting to hear that your colleagues think that you are either brilliant or an idiot. You need to respond in such a fashion that indicates that you seriously take on board what colleagues say and how much you enjoy and respect your work colleagues. This leads to a more productive environment.

ANSWER1: I would expect them to say that I am hard working, professional and loyal. I always solicit feedback from my colleagues both formally through our company's 360 degree review process and also informally throughout the life of the projects we work on. If it is in anyway negative, I am objective and take on board what was said.

ANSWER2: When you work closely with people all day, it is very important to have a bond and a team focused mentality to be more productive. I expect my colleagues to point out any issues or negative feedback that they may have with me and I work to improve based on the feedback for the purpose of progression.

ANSWER3: I really do believe that colleagues would recognize both the strength of my leadership and my team playing abilities. I have worked hard at both and always respected feedback over the years to make me a stronger colleague and person in general.

∾

Can you give an example of your leadership qualities?

ANALYSIS: Leadership comes in many guises. They are looking for you to acknowledge that you have such skills and give some concrete examples where you have led in either the workplace or externally.

ANSWER1: I have no issue with taking responsibility and being accountable for a project or process. At my last role, I ran the quality assurance team. We had to ensure that the product was as perfect as it could be before it left the plant. At certain times, I had to send the product back to the line for improvement and had no issue with pushing back on management to have it re-produced.

ANSWER2: I am always the first to put up my hand for a leadership role at the work place. As is evident from my resume, I have led many teams successfully across many different projects. I was school captain for two years in high school. I like to lead by example.

ANSWER3: Career progression is synonymous with leadership in my mind. The company's growth plan that you have outlined requires strong leaders. I have a very strong track record; I led the team in a recent high profile case against a competitor. We spent many hours and touched on a range of emotions but I managed to keep everyone focused and we attained the result we were looking for.

ᏇᎧ

Have you ever led a team?

ANALYSIS: The answer may be 'No' but of course that does not mean you are unwilling or incapable of doing so. In reality, the chances are that you have led a team at some stage in your life either at work or externally. Have you assembled a number of people for a function ever? That is an example of leading a team.

ANSWER1: No, I have not officially led a team yet as I was on the road as a solo salesman in my previous and only role. I would really relish the opportunity to be a member of and to lead a team. I feel it is possible to achieve a lot more under a team structure rather than in isolation. I believe that I could transform many of the disadvantages of solo selling to be advantages in the team environment.

ANSWER2: Yes, I have led many teams and really enjoy it. I am a true believer in the team structure and its value it brings both to the employees and the organization. The key is to keep the team motivated and to always lead from the front. I actively encourage openness and idea generation from each of the team members.

ANSWER3: I worked in a very competitive environment for many years. It was really a dog-eat dog culture and this was perpetuated by the lack of team culture. Everyone was out for oneself but that gained only very short-term success for company and was its ultimate doom. I am therefore a huge advocate of team building and believe it is kernel to company growth.

↝

What is the largest team you have led?

ANALYSIS: Note that you do not need to have had 500 people reporting to you. Many organizations depend on people being able to effectively reach across defined departmental lines to move the company forwards. Therefore, you may have unwittingly led a much larger team than you thought.

ANSWER1: I led a team of two hundred people in my last project. It was a multi-year project based on regulatory requirements so failure was not an option. To add to the complexity, many of the team was off-shored in India. I created a tight layer of management around me who contained the right skill set to execute the plan. We delivered the project on time and on budget. The experience honed my leadership management skills such as communicating, creating and executing strategies.

ANSWER2: I led a team who did not all report to me directly. It was a cross-departmental initiative mandated by senior management. Leading a virtual team can be tricky as many do not report to either to me or to my department. However, I did manage to get buy in from everyone at the beginning, gaining trust for my vision and the project was ultimately a success. I could not have done this without having a full arsenal of leadership skills.

ANSWER3: I led the ice hockey team in college. I learned some very valuable team lessons that I have carried through to my work life. In any team, there are many different personalities and viewpoints. As the leader of the team, I had to channel all these characteristics into one strong and forceful entity. We didn't win the championship but we were very proud of our efforts. My teammates applauded me for my skills as captain.

৩

Have you ever spoken at conferences?

ANALYSIS: They want to know if you have any issues with public speaking as one of the aspects of the role maybe to promote the company externally. If you have never had the opportunity to speak at a conference, it is doesn't mean you have issues with public speaking.

ANSWER1: I have spoken at industry conferences and I believe that many of my presentations are publicly available on the Internet. I find that speaking at conferences is another form of marketing for the company. It helps position the company as a market leader. Valuable business contacts are made at these conferences.

ANSWER2: I haven't had the opportunity to speak at such a venue but would love to. I have no fear of public speaking and I feel that it would be an honor to represent the company at a conference. This also appears to be great way to network and keep abreast of industry developments. My current company is too small to support attending these.

ANSWER3: I have prepared material for my boss who is a regular conference speaker. Indeed, I have been to many conferences and am usually in charge of the company booth in the presentation hall. I would love to be on one of the panels or speak on an industry topic as I am very in tune with what is going right now in the industry.

ॐ

How adept at technology are you?

ANALYSIS: Technology plays a huge role in all business these days. They will need to be convinced that you can handle the basics such as word processing and spreadsheets for nearly all roles. IT and Engineering roles will generate more specific and incisive questions on this.

ANSWER1: Technical proficiency in this day and age is a must regardless of what profession you are in. The days of the just depending on the IT department alone are finished. I am very proficient with spreadsheets, word processing and presentation software. These are key tools for me to effectively execute my business.

ANSWER2: The companies that are nudging ahead in the industry are the ones that have adopted technology to make their business more profitable. With a more astute customer base and tighter profit margin, phrases like straight through processing and front to back flow are becoming more commonplace. I am very familiar with these concepts.

ANSWER3: I learned some basic programming skills in college and am very familiar with how social networking sites have managed to make the world a smaller place. Every industry is following suit and using technology to make their companies a smaller place, train their employees in company practices, cut costs through IT efficiency and keep ahead of both the competition and industry regulation.

 ∾

Are you a big picture or a detailed person?

ANALYSIS: The interviewers want to know if you are willing to get your hands dirty if needs be. They expect to hear that you can be relied upon to be both. They do not want to hire someone just to draw some diagrams on a board.

ANSWER1: I believe that in order to be a strategist, you must have one time been a detailed person. As I moved up the ladder, I have become more involved with designing strategy and driving the company forward. However, I do keep my hand in on the details of what is driving the industry and what changes we need to implement.

ANSWER2: My Company is a small one so we are all required to get involved in the low level detail. This does not bother me as we are equipped to make strategic decisions on the back of this detail. The trick is to balance your workday and week to benefit from all levels of experience required to run the business.

ANSWER3: The role on offer here is a senior management role and from the description it is mainly strategic in nature. I have worked for many years in the trenches and feel very equipped to make strategic decisions. Due to my experience, I do know where to go to find the detail required to make such strategic decisions.

᠎

How do you keep up with developments in the industry?

ANALYSIS: If you have been out of the industry for a while or if this is your first job, it is vital that you demonstrate that you are up to date on the current developments be they, regulation, new products or macroeconomic issues. This will strengthen your claim to be committed to the industry and therefore the company.

ANSWER1: I am still very much in touch with movements in the industry as I have retained my subscription to many related magazines, blogs and email services. For example, I am fully up to speed on the new regulations that will change the way we do business if they are successfully passed by the government.

ANSWER2: I have been in the industry so long that it is very hard to lose touch. I have many friends and ex-colleagues whom I meet regularly and who keep me up to date. Therefore, I am very much aware what the issues are with your competitors right now especially those who are losing and will continue to lose personnel over the next six months.

ANSWER3: I feel that in an ever-evolving industry like ours, it is imperative to be up to date with the latest innovations, issues and regulations. I use a mixture of media ranging from industry magazines to industry specific websites to keep abreast of developing items. Of course the biggest change is about to occur in two months time when the international trade agreement begins.

∽

Why did your previous firm not live up to your expectations?

ANALYSIS: Obviously if your previous firm went bankrupt then the initial answer is easy. An interview is supposed to be a positive experience for the interviewer. If you are really aggrieved with your previous company and the way things ended up there, keep a lid on it. The chances are your previous company has not met your expectations (by the very fact that you are here). Use this to promote the reason why you want to join this company and why you expect it to live up to your expectations.

ANSWER1: At some stage in everyone's career you need to assess where you are going and if the current path is leading to where you want to be. My current firm is great, very successful in its niche and to that extent has lived up to my expectations. However, I want to grow beyond this niche and bring my experience to a bigger company where I can make a difference.

ANSWER2: I have always had a great experience with my company. Unfortunately, the industry and therefore the demand for our core products have fallen dramatically. At this point the company will be filing for bankruptcy. Of course, this in itself is a great learning experience, one that I would like to build on with a great company like yours.

ANSWER3: The Company overhauled management in the past six months based on advice from a highly regarded management consultancy. Senior management is now implementing the changes and a number of us feel that the changes do not fit the ethos of the company. This company is structured more like the previous one and I feel this is the right structure to breed success as you have shown to date.

❦

What are some of the structural changes you would make to this company?

ANALYSIS: Are you someone who can instigate change? This is forefront in the interviewer's mind. The majority of hires are expected to come fresh with ideas to a company and drive it forwards. You may not fully know the whole structure of the company but come prepared with examples of previous changes and propositions. This question is aimed at someone coming in at a very high management level.

ANSWER1: The more nimble the management layer, the more efficient the company. I always operate with a thin management layer, functionally aligned with the core production processes of the company. I would need to assess the management layer at this company before drawing any conclusions.

ANSWER2: I am very keen on bottom up analysis. I believe that it is important that every function and its contribution to the company's return on investment are fully understood. I would need to spend some time analyzing this. Naturally, some departments are not directly aligned with productivity but serve a horizontal function across all the units. These departments would need to be included in a matrix analysis.

ANSWER3: Senior management directs the company's ethos, reputation, production and its success. I look for very strong senior managers who want to lead by example. I expect a senior manager to perform well every year and to be compensated on his or her most recent work. I know some of the managers here already and have a sense that the standards are high but there is always room for improvement so I would expect some re-shuffling.

❧

Have you ever over engineered a solution beyond the obvious answer?

ANALYSIS: You probably have but this is something that comes with experience. They want to know how you would identify that you were going down the wrong path and what you would do to mitigate this. How do you balance a quick solution given budget constraints with a more strategic solution?

ANSWER1: The ability to spot an obvious solution comes with experience. I believe earlier on in my career that I may have been guilty of over analyzing solutions to the nth degree. However, as I progressed, I accumulated my experiences and applied them to each new task with more efficiency.

ANSWER2: The great thing about teamwork is that you will always have a mix of people, experience and opinion. Some people are very theoretical; this may due to their academic or early career background. I have a very pragmatic approach to work and therefore rarely over engineer solutions.

ANSWER3: Some careers demand that you be absolutely meticulous and there is no way around this. In this industry, you cannot be a maverick but you must strive to multi-task, network and re-apply solutions you have learned elsewhere. This will speed up delivery and lessen any over engineering.

෴

Give me an example of a time when you showed initiative in the work place?

ANALYSIS: You always need to show initiative in the workplace. They want to know that you understand that. Every day will present a new problem that needs to be solved. You can show initiative in many ways, have an example or two ready but importantly, let them know that you know that initiative is necessary.

ANSWER1: I think it is necessary to show initiative every day. A new unique problem arises every day and that is what I love about work. Yesterday, we had an irate client complaining via email about his perception of our delivery times. I jumped in my car and drove two and a half hours to discuss the issues with him face to face. He was surprised but appreciative of my initiative.

ANSWER2: During the boom time we purchased many servers without really putting much of a control process around it. I took the initiative to implement a capacity program. Instead of buying new servers, capacity on existing servers were shared and re-used. This program saved us millions.

ANSWER3: I felt that employee morale was low or at the very least we needed sometime outside the office to get to know each other and our families. I find that the more you know about someone, the more productive you will be. I started "family night" where we all chipped in some money and the company matched. We did this every two months and it was very fruitful.

CHAPTER 3: THE COMPANY AND THE ROLE IN QUESTION

Introduction

There are always interview questions about the company you are applying to. They will expect you to have researched the company and the role.

The more you know, the more impressed the interviewer will be. There is nothing more annoying for an interviewer than suspecting that you have no idea about the job you applied for. Expect interview questions that endeavor to discover whether you have researched the role or not.

You are not expected to know everything prior to the interview but ensure that you know something about the role.

∾

What is it about the company that attracts you here?

ANALYSIS: How well do you know this Company? Where do we stand in this industry? Do you know our products and results? Do you know people working here? Why do you want to work here and in this industry? The interviewers will be proud of their company and in some cases will think it is the best place on earth. But what made you apply exactly?

ANSWER1: The Company has a great reputation in and outside this industry. I believe that it has a great platform for career growth. The pedigree of staff you have working for you is second to none. This is borne true by the continuous growth the company has had over the past few years.

ANSWER2: The startup formation is very attractive to me. My entrepreneurial skills really flourish in that environment. I agree with your vision and my research indicates that the product niche you are working towards is going to be a winner.

ANSWER3: This industry has been under a lot of scrutiny from both the regulators and the media in general. I believe that it is a really exciting time now and a great chance to position oneself for growth. This company should flourish at a time like this and position itself to be a market leader over the next few years. It has the right approach, ethos and business model to do so.

What do you know about the company?

ANALYSIS: You will be expected to know something about the company, its products and financials. Try to read as much you can online or get the most recent annual report. Failure to know something will indicate a complete lack of interest (rightfully or wrongfully).

ANSWER1: As you are a private company, it is difficult to obtain annual reports and disclosures. However, I did find some great commentary on you on the internet and I also followed up with some ex employees. All have re-affirmed my positive opinion of the company and its approach to business.

ANSWER2: I have read thoroughly the available financial reports and media PR for the past few years. Your track record is very impressive and what you have achieved in a short period of time is unparalleled. Just walking through your reception this morning, I could sense the employee camaraderie and dynamism.

ANSWER3: I have followed the success of this company for many years. I am very familiar with all your products and services. I subscribe to your company updates online. It is very impressive how you continuously keep ahead of the competition in terms of innovation and employee retention.

Tell me something positive you have heard about the company?

ANALYSIS: Show that you have done some research and heard positive things regarding the quality of its products, staff training, retention rates or management rotation program. It is always good to impress why you think this company is the one for you.

ANSWER1: Absolutely! I know many people who work here now and have done so in the past. Everyone rates the company a fantastic place to work. Employees are a firm's best asset and it is good to hear such positive accolades.

ANSWER2: I have read numerous articles on your ambitious expansion plans for the next five years. It is very positive that even in this environment, your company has the foresight, resources and confidence to continue to expand its product and service range.

ANSWER3: Your products and financial returns speak for themselves. The one recurring positive theme is your ability to motivate and challenge your employees. Your employee rotation training program is one of the most attractive in the industry and has received positive accolades from all those who have been lucky to participate.

Have you ever heard anything negative about this company?

ANALYSIS: You may have and if it is well known or publicized in the media, you are somewhat obliged to mention it. However, put a positive spin on it and say that you understand that the company has moved on and that is why you are attracted to it.

ANSWER1: I haven't heard anything negative at all. Even if I had, it would still not put me off applying for a role here. The overriding success and the high employee morale outweigh any potential negatives in my mind.

ANSWER2: The high profile suit taken by an ex employee has been publicized in the media over the past few weeks. I have not let that sway my interest in the company. Every individual is different and will always have an unique experience with his or her employer. I am not going to allow someone else's experience determine mine.

ANSWER3: I am aware of the class action suit by a number of people who bought your last product. However, my research also shows me that this suit only represents five per cent of the customers who purchased the product. I think that companies will always have some form of negativity to deal with; this is just a part of business.

What changes would you make to the company?

ANALYSIS: You may have some good ideas outside the remit of the role. Don't be afraid to mention them. In many cases, the company may already have tried what you are suggesting but you are showing a keen entrepreneurial spirit that will be impressive.

ANSWER1: I followed the success of your company for a very long time and am very respectful of the progress made to date. I believe that every new employee should bring with him new ideas and a different perspective to the business model. I fully expect that after a brief period of assessment, I will be in a position to suggest and implement changes.

ANSWER2: This industry is ever evolving and to remain competitive everyone needs to evolve. Evolution means change and I have a number of marketing strategies that I truly believe will help your product move up the leader board. I have been immersed in the marketing of such products for 5 years and would like to pitch some different approaches to you.

ANSWER3: I may be fresh out of school, but one of my courses covered in detail the concept of change management. Many companies are now recognizing this as a function in it of itself and it is easy to see why. We have seen so much technology change in the last couple of years from social networks to blogs. I can see a use for these within any company to disseminate information internally effectively and efficiently. I would like to be involved in making these changes.

Do you think that your recent experience is relevant to this role?

ANALYSIS: It really depends on the level of entry. If you are a very junior person with just a couple of year's experience, it is not as important. If you are more senior, there will be an expectancy that you have relevant experience. However, you should also leave room to show what change you can bring to the new company.

ANSWER1: You have provided me with a very comprehensive overview of the role. It sounds like the person who was doing this has done a very good job in evolving the role and increasing the profile of the function with the company. I would look to solidify that and also make the function more integrated into the company's kernel processes.

ANSWER2: There have been a lot of industry changes recently and I am aware that competition has become more aggressive in this sector. I will make some changes in your process to better streamline production and reduce costs. This will bring the company more in line with the competition.

ANSWER3: This role is not what it was 2 years and I would not expect it to be the same in another 2 years. This is a very dynamic time in the industry with the advent of online social networking. We need to take advantage of technical evolution. I intend to adopt this into my changes.

∽

What attracts you to the position?

ANALYSIS: They really want to know if you know what you are interviewing for? There is nothing more annoying to an interviewer than a candidate who has not fully researched the role by themselves or with their recruiter. Make sure you have gone at length to clarify the position and where it sits in the organization before you walk in the door. Ideally, you have had a full debrief either from your recruiting agent, someone in the company or from an ex colleague familiar with the company and position. Be sure to project at all times that you are fully aware what position you are interviewing for.

ANSWER1: I have been following the progress of your company for quite some time now. When this role was presented to me, I immediately saw a good fit based on my background. The number of years experience, the level of understanding and the deep knowledge of the industry all speak to my experience. Also the future direction of the role is in line with where I would like my career to go.

ANSWER2: I haven't been actively looking for a new job, as the only position that would interest me is one that would provide more challenge and opportunity. Your advertisement jumped out at me and I immediately became excited about the prospect of working here. This was consolidated further when I conducted some more research into the position and the synergies with my experience became more apparent.

ANSWER3: I have been presented with opportunities to change role both internally and externally for a few years. The reason I never followed through was that I felt that the roles were too similar in nature to my current position. I can see that this role will provide a career challenge for me and that is something I am really keen on. Your growth path is unique and the stated opportunity to diversify into another sector within the company is really a great chance at my level.

ᘓ

Why should I hire you over the other well-qualified candidates?

ANALYSIS: Whether there are other candidates is irrelevant – they are looking for you to sell your skills to them. This is your interview and not that of other candidates, be very clear and positive about the benefits of hiring you. You do not need to compare yourself to others – in your mind, you don't have to.

ANSWER1: I have fully researched both this role and the company and believe that it is an excellent opportunity. My direct experience is absolutely relevant to this role. Not only will I be able to hit the ground running but also implement changes to help evolve this role within the organization.

ANSWER2: I have successfully implemented change and increased productivity substantially at my last two firms. I have never lost the hunger and the desire to rise to the next challenge. This role presents me with that challenge and I am really hoping that we can work together to succeed for this firm.

ANSWER3: I am perfectly suited to this role because I share the vision you have for the company and know how to achieve it. Growing a nascent company and formulating an exit strategy is something that I have done many times over. I understand the emotions involved and possess the mentality and the skill to execute this plan together.

಄

Do you think that you are qualified for the position?

ANALYSIS: Of course you are and the fact that they are interviewing you implies that the company thinks you are as well. Even if there is a small part of you that feels you do not possess some part of the requisite experience, don't go there. This is your job and that is how you need to think.

ANSWER1: Yes absolutely, I have had many years of direct experience with this product in a number of companies. I know the industry, the products, the competition and the regulation extremely well. I understand exactly what problem you are trying to solve and I have the tools to implement the solution for you.

ANSWER2: My team building and problem solving track record qualify me for this role. I will be able to make a difference immediately. You have been very clear on what you expect from the role and where you want to take this company. I would relish the opportunity to put my skills to use here.

ANSWER3: As this is a graduate entry role, I believe that I am as qualified as anyone in terms of my relevant academic qualifications. In addition, I have also spent some working for free at one of your competitors and have kept abreast of all the changes in the market place over the past few years. My extracurricular activities have allowed me to build on leadership and networking skills that would be very useful for this role.

∽

Aren't you over qualified for this role?

ANALYSIS: Of course, that may be true. They are asking if you are willing to step back into this role. You should be willing to step back in the short term to move forward in the long term. You do not need to apologize for your experience. If this was a real concern, they would not be interviewing in the first place.

ANSWER1: Well, I certainly am qualified and my knowledge and experience in this area would be a very valuable addition to your team. Likewise, I do see areas where I can also be challenged and learn more. In that sense, I do not believe that I am over qualified.

ANSWER2: Every situation and company is unique. While I definitely have the right qualification for this role, you have outlined that your company has a very different approach to this market. Therefore someone with my experience would have to adapt his skills to this different approach, which would be a very interesting challenge.

ANSWER3: My goals are not short term. While there are some similarities with a subset of my experience for this role, I tend to look at the long-term prospects here. The career growth you have outlined is second to none and that is what I am aiming for in a number of years down the road.

❧

Are you willing to start on a lesser role and we can re-assess later?

ANALYSIS: They like your resume and are testing how badly you want to join the company. As an interview process evolves, companies see fits for the candidates beyond the advertised roles so do not be put off by such a question. Be positive and ensure that you are open to this with an understanding that the longer-term prospects are in line with your expectations.

ANSWER1: Everyone has been very open with me about the role and the level it is at. It still interests me, as I know I can evolve this into something bigger and make you the market leader in this industry. I relish the opportunity to work here and take this role to the next level.

ANSWER2: I am open to discussions about other roles. It appears that you have a very strong career growth program so I assume that all positions would benefit from this. I am looking for my next ten years of employment so a role deemed to be a lesser one in the short-term does not bother me.

ANSWER3: As this is a startup, I am not sure that there is such thing as a lesser role! Basically everyone has to do a bit of everything and work hard to get this company off the ground.

I believe that you can still learn something in any role and you need to keep looking forward.

ᘓ

Why should I not hire you?

ANALYSIS: They are trying to catch you off guard. Of course they should hire you and you are here to let them know that. There is no doubt in your mind that you are the best. Give them some reasons why they should hire you but don't be arrogant.

ANSWER1: I am sure that a great opportunity like this has attracted many suitable candidates from the industry. I believe that both my academic qualifications and career achievements speak for themselves. In addition, I am still hungry to make a difference and implement change.

ANSWER1: If you were not to hire me, I think we would both have lost an opportunity. I would bring many years of experience to this role and have many views on how to expand your product line, reduce the cost basis and increase your revenues. I have a proven track record and would love to work with you on this expansion.

ANSWER2: Your Company has made many strides in recent years and is really well positioned to be a leader in this industry. My current company dominates the market but has become very fat in size and that is hurting its growth potential. I have been through the growing pains before and would be a great addition to your strong team. I believe that these are reasons to hire me.

ANSWER3: I am sure that a great opportunity like this has attracted many suitable candidates from the industry. I believe that both my academic qualifications and career achievements speak for themselves. In addition, I am hungry to make a difference and implement change. I would not present myself for interview unless I was one hundred per cent certain that I could fulfill this role.

∽

What happens if you don't get this role?

ANALYSIS: They want to see if you are so desperate to get out of your current role that you will try to get any job. They expect to hear that this is really job you are interested in and if you are unsuccessful, you will need to take a step back and re-evaluate.

ANSWER1: I am a very positive thinker and don't tend to analyze situations which may or may not arise. I have been very impressed by everyone who I have met here and with the openness with respect to the role. I would be disappointed if I was not a fit as I think, based on my experience and career ambitions, this would be a perfect position for me.

ANSWER2: As I mentioned, I am talking to one or two other companies. But I feel that this role is the one for me and even if I were to be offered a position from one of the other companies, it would be difficult to accept knowing what I do about this one. If I prove unsuccessful here, I would ask for some feedback as to what you felt I was missing so I could re-apply at a later date.

ANSWER3: I promised myself that I would only apply for something that I thought was a real career builder. I haven't applied for a role for two years on that account. This role really ticks all the boxes and I believe it would be a great fit mutually. Should I be unsuccessful, I will stay where I am and keep an eye out for a similar opening at a later date.

෧ᢣ

Your title would be different here – is that an issue?

ANALYSIS: All companies have some differences in corporate structure and management layering. The interviewer is really testing to see what is more important to you – a title or the role and the potential that it brings with it. You are here to prove that you really want the job, and that the role and its potential rates above title.

ANSWER1: Title is the furthest thing from my mind. The nature of the role and the challenge is more important to me. This role is the natural next step for someone with my experience and whatever the internal title is, I am willing to accept it. I think people sometimes tend to get too caught up on titles while I prefer to focus on the role.

ANSWER2: There is a lot of disparity in the industry with respect to titles and indeed some places don't have any. Title is not overly important to me. I believe that if you consistently produce and grow your career then you will be rewarded accordingly. I don't need a title to tell me how well I am doing.

ANSWER3: As this is a startup company, I can only assume that titles are pretty meaningless. Previously when I worked at a start up, we made up our own titles! The aim is for everyone to work together to make this venture as successful as possible. If someone is concerned about a title then may I suggest that they are focusing on the wrong issue?

❧

If we made you an offer right now – would you accept?

ANALYSIS: They are trying to find out how badly you want this role in this company. The question usually stems from one of two reasons; Firstly, for some reason they are not convinced that you have made up your mind about this company or you are still weighing up your options or secondly, they may think that you are absolutely perfect for this role.

Note that the common case is the first one and again you will need to convince them that you fully understand the role and really want this job.

ANSWER1: Yes absolutely, this interview process has cleared up any questions I had and I can see the advantages of working here over some of your competitors. Everyone I met here has impressed me and all have an ambition to succeed. I am very open to starting negotiations right now if that what it would take to work here.

ANSWER2: I have no doubt in my mind that this role and company can offer me a fantastic career path. I am quite happy to accept an offer today if we can reach an agreement. I would be prepared to cancel any other interviews I have.

ANSWER3: I made up my mind some time back that this is where I want to be. Any comparison with other companies in this sector indicates that this is the strongest enterprise around on many levels ranging from career growth to work environment. I would be delighted if you offered me a role today.

෯

How do you rate this interview?

ANALYSIS: A reaction question and they are trying to catch you off guard so best to be prepared! They will want to hear about the useful information you have heard and expect that you are now more familiar with both the role and the company. Therefore the interview has been enjoyable and informative.

ANSWER1: This is a very useful and thorough interview. You have concisely and succinctly outlined the role, the company's ambitions and the next steps. Many interviewers fail to portray this and I thank you for the time and effort you have put into this.

ANSWER2: I have experienced many rigid interviews in the past and in most cases I have left with some uncertainty in my mind. I appreciate your candidness and frankness. For me, this proves that there is openness in your company's approach to work and employee development.

ANSWER3: I have thoroughly enjoyed speaking with you today. I had some open questions about the role and company policy but you have given me even more insight than I expected. I believe the role is a great fit for me and I look forward to continuing the discussion with your team.

෨ට

Do you have questions for me?

ANALYSIS: If you don't, they will think that you are not that interested. Interviewers find it rude when interviewees have no questions. Even if this is the tenth interview with the same company, have a few questions (even if you know the answers)!

ANSWER1: I have met five people at the company now and have a very clear idea of what the role entails and the career progression. You mentioned that you are here fifteen years and have progressed to the top. Do you believe that someone coming in laterally at my rank will be able to progress quickly through the company?

ANSWER2: What are the plans for expansion over the next few years? I read that you have some plans so I am curious to hear your view on this. In addition, could you outline how this role would play a part in this expansion? I am very keen that this role will be involved in the next wave of company and product development.

ANSWER3: You mentioned that the company encourages movement across regions. Can you elaborate more on that program and if that opportunity is open to someone in this role? Also, I am really attracted to the career flexibility the company allows. Can you also elaborate on the cross departmental program?

CHAPTER 4: BEHAVIORAL QUESTIONS

Introduction

All interviews these days have some behavioral questions. This category will cover some piercing questions without pushing legal boundaries. The interviewer will delve into your relationships with colleagues, your boss and your clients.

Essentially they want to know how you behave in the work place and if you have any issues that may cloud your judgment on occasion. Your answers to the questions should prove that you are of sound deposition and understand the importance of a team orientated work environment.

෴

Have you ever fired anyone?

ANALYSIS: Firing or making people redundant is an ugly but realistic side of business. They need to know that you understand this and as you progress are willing to step up to make these difficult decisions. If you have been fortunate enough to avoid having to do this, you will still need to let them know that you understand the necessity of such action on occasion.

ANSWER1: I never had to fire anyone but I do understand it is sometimes necessary. If the situation arose, I would step up to the plate and take the appropriate action as required.

ANSWER2: In our last firm, our productivity fell substantial due to increased competition. We needed to downsize. I had to fire people whom I had worked alongside for a very long time. I am not going to pretend that it was easy but I understood that it was a necessary business decision and I carried out the re-structuring as required.

ANSWER3: I had to fire a disruptive colleague at my first firm. He was constantly late for work and tardy in reaching agreed milestones. I followed the HR process completely before firing him. This was a necessary move for team morale and company production.

Describe a situation where you identified and mitigated a risk?

ANALYSIS: Every problem has a solution and they want to know that you have the ability to identify a problem. Also, you should always put yourself in a position to try to solve the issue. There is nothing worse than dismissing a problem as someone else's.

ANSWER1: I was asked to take over a project that was mid lifecycle. I reviewed the progress to date and the plans. I quickly identified that the project was going to run out of money three months before the end date. I designed a strategy to outsource some of the development to more cost effective locations.

ANSWER2: We had a really tight knit team and senior management was impressed with our performance. We had been together awhile. I noticed that one member of the team became more introverted and I knew something was wrong. I approached her after work and she was embarrassed to tell me that another company wanted her to join them. She was feeling un-challenged in her current role and therefore was considering leaving the team. I subtly changed her role to provide her with the challenge she wanted and she remained as productive as ever.

ANSWER3: We ran an online business selling various books and equipment to golf enthusiasts. The IT infrastructure was all developed internally as we wanted to retain control. I noticed on occasion that the site slowed down but nobody knew why. I discovered a server memory leak and commissioned IT to build a monitoring tool that allowed us to track memory usage easily so we could increase memory when needed.

ᕽᕽ

How do you deal with failure?

ANALYSIS: Failure has many definitions. The source or gravity of the failure is not what they are questioning you on. You or someone else may feel you failed in a particular task. What did you learn from this? How did you bounce back? Do you feel stronger for it?

ANSWER1: I tend to be quite hard on myself as a rule. When things went wrong, I used to get quite annoyed with myself. As I have matured and become more experienced, I find that I now see every perceived failure as another learning opportunity and assess what went wrong and how to avoid it in the future.

ANSWER2: I used to work for a very demanding boss. He would bark orders and had unrealistic expectations on delivery schedules. We all used to feel like failures. I learned how to manage his expectations and negotiate with him with respect to timescales and delivery. I helped him to help us and there was an improvement all round.

ANSWER3: Everyone in life will have to deal with failure at different levels. I was dropped from the football team in school. I was very annoyed and could not believe it. After about a week of sulking, I approached the coach, asked what was wrong and could I do better? I trained harder, won my place back and in retrospect the coach taught me a lesson.

୧୬

What happens if people on your team are not pulling their weight?

ANALYSIS: They are testing your human management and conflict resolution skills. They are not interested in hiring someone who is simply going to fire anyone who is not pulling their weight. You will need to show that you are willing to mentor employees and give them every chance to succeed.

ANSWER1: Conflict resolution is very important in the work place. If a person is not pulling their weight then that is a conflict. It is important to let a person know when they are not performing, as otherwise you are doing them and the team a disservice. Everyone should get a second chance. If the behavior persists then more drastic action would be called for.

ANSWER2: People who were previously great producers may not be pulling their weight at the present time. It is important to understand what has de-motivated this person. It may be personal issues, burn out or unhappiness with other team members. Understanding the reason is the best way to resolve the problem.

ANSWER3: There is nothing more problematic in a team environment than a member not pulling their weight. As a manager, I am obliged to rectify this. It may be the case that I have not understood this person's skill set, and then I need to carefully reorganize the team without disenfranchising other members. If that is not possible then I need to find another role for that person outside the team.

❧

How do you establish a rapport with clients or customers?

ANALYSIS: Without customers or clients, there is no business. Some roles will be more customer/client facing than others. They want to know that you understand this and that you are willing to follow a code when it comes to dealing with customers no matter how frustrating it can be on occasion.

ANSWER1: Customer satisfaction is kernel to this business. I am a great advocate of open dialog with my customers. I like to involve them at every stage of the process so they have buy-in. Even if things are not going exactly to plan, I want them to know. I believe that they respect the openness.

ANSWER2: I take client meetings and entertainment very seriously. I don't simply just send email updates but I make a point of visiting my client once a quarter regardless of where they are situated and take them for nights out. Without the customer, there is no business so I see these meetings as an investment in the business.

ANSWER3: I worked in a small family run business where I really learned the value of customer service. I found that the human touch went a long way. For example knowing the names of the customer's kids, their ages or what schools they go to shows the client that you have interest in them and their needs.

∽

How long does it take you to reach a decision?

ANALYSIS: You will be faced with many decisions, some immediate, and others that will take more time. They need to hear that you are willing to make decisions and also how you would make those decisions. You want to prove that you are decisive without giving the impression that you can be a loose cannon who makes wild decisions with no basis.

ANSWER 1: I am very decisive by nature and I believe that it is a critical leadership quality. My decisions are made based on experience and client expectations. The gravity of each decision depends on the situation. Sometimes, it is necessary to assess a situation completely while other times decisions can be made more quickly – it depends on the importance. For example, when a project is running potentially over budget, I will step in and take the measures required to put it back on track.

ANSWER 2: Everyone, no matter what level they are at is faced with making decisions. If I am working in a team environment, I solicit feedback from everyone who is key to the process and then I make a decision, sometimes it has to be a compromise but I am not afraid to make the decision. The IT department has looked to me for functional decisions in the past. I have made these based on my own view and that of the key team members.

ANSWER3: I was faced with a very difficult decision when deciding which school to go to. I had a week to decide. Therefore, I had to quickly analyze the pros and cons of both the academic and the extracurricular activities of each school on which to base my decision. The real lesson I learned was that once you make a decision, you should not torture yourself by looking back months later and wishing you had made a different one, but instead objectively evaluate the outcome of the decision and learn from the process.

∞

How do you establish credibility with your team?

ANALYSIS: They expect that at some stage you will be looking to take a leadership role. The interviewers want to see how you expect to establish yourself as a leader, especially when you are new to a company. You need to be able to extract the best from a team but that does not mean that you have to be the most knowledgeable on every topic.

ANSWER1: It is best to be realistic with respect to expectations for your team when trying to build credibility. Your team needs to believe in you just as much as you need to believe in your team. Above all your team needs to trust you and know that they will be rewarded accordingly in terms of career growth, promotion and compensation should they do a good job for you. I always bat for my team and I have a reputation for doing that, therefore people always want to work for me.

ANSWER2: At the outset of any project, I have a roundtable with the team. Everyone has to pitch a view and it creates a strong sense of ownership amongst everyone. I believe that credibility is built by showing the team that you respect them, their input and opinions to the process. It is important to recognize that each member brings something unique to the team and also continuous motivation and feedback is appreciated.

ANSWER3: In business, losing the respect of your team is a huge mistake. A de-motivated team will cause problems not only for you but also the project and the company. Team morale needs to be high even in times of crisis. You need to let the team know that you are a part of the team, will stand up for them in crisis, and lead from the front so they can learn from you. Team bonding events such as nights out are a very effective way of harnessing a team's culture and credibility.

෴

What is the best way to communicate with management?

ANALYSIS: The ability to condense a topic into a few key sentences is a very important requirement in the workplace. Everyone has a boss and everyone has to do this. You need to show them that you can summarize issues quickly and efficiently.

ANSWER1: Senior Managers are busy people and you usually only have a few minutes to get your point across. I summarize any meetings with a list of issues and actions. If there is a problem, I always like to go with a proposal containing both the problem and solution. Sometimes management overrides it but they appreciate the input.

ANSWER2: Knowing your manager and his or her expectations is key to successful communications. Some managers want to be involved in the minutiae - others are more high level. I use different medium for each. Detailed email communication for those who want it at that detailed level and more of a bullet point summary for the more high-level.

ANSWER3: Keeping the manager updated at all times is of utmost importance. As a manager myself, I need to be aware of progress and more importantly the issues. If there is something urgent, then pick up the phone or walk into his/her office. Do not let any issues grow larger without him/her knowing. For more regular and passive updates, you can use email that he/she can read at their leisure.

❧

What happens when results are not up to your manager's expectations?

ANALYSIS: You will not always get the result you are looking for and at times you will have to compromise on an outcome. They want to know how you communicate and react in such situations. In addition, they expect that this is a learning experience for you.

ANSWER1: I am very upfront with my boss at the beginning of any project with respect to his expectations. I learned this very early in my career when I was too eager to over impress and subsequently mismanaged his expectations by delivering something that was way off target. That has never happened again.

ANSWER2: The ability to manage expectations is a challenge and a skill that everyone needs to learn in their career. Your boss is a busy person and depends on you to have the initiative to develop, lead and manage his expectations. If you are given a task, you need to check in with your boss every so often to give progress reports so if there are any issues, they can be addressed early in the process.

ANSWER3: There needs to be a layer of trust between you and your boss. That trust is achieved by strong job performance and feedback. If results are not up to your manager's expectation, you must learn why and analyze what you could have done better so you improve the next time and add to the trust.

∽

Have you ever been unhappy with your own performance on a project?

ANALYSIS: We are constantly learning and should want to improve. They want to know that you recognize that each project is unique and there will always be something you can do better. You don't have to be unhappy with your effort but just be aware what you and your team learned through the process.

ANSWER1: I like to review my work periodically as each role I perform has some unique attributes. I see each performance as a building block in my career. I always want to be learning so I do on occasion spot areas for improvement that I channel into my learning process.

ANSWER2: I encourage my colleagues and myself to consistently improve. Improvement means better communication, better planning, better understanding of what the industry and competitors are doing, more efficient processes and better client experience. I don't believe that I have ever been unhappy per se but always am working on improvement.

ANSWER3: I have actually. I was a business analyst on a project in my first job about ten years ago. I was given a task to define the requirements for a new sales process and I decided to work in isolation and not reach out to experienced staff for help. It was a grave mistake that I never repeated and I have learned the art of analysis, thorough requirement definition, communication, team playing and lifecycle management.

സ

What kind of boss do you work best for?

ANALYSIS: Every boss is unique and everyone has his or her quirks. They are really asking what kind of boss you are or aspire to be. What are the skills and qualities of a good boss ranging from clear objective setting, to team building, employee motivation and career planning?

ANSWER1: I view the boss-employee relationship as a two-way partnership. I want to help my boss and I want him/her to help me to help him/her. Therefore, I expect my boss to have clear objectives for me and give me semi-annual reviews. I do not need to be micro-managed but need high-level guidance.

ANSWER2: I like my boss to be a good listener and as motivated as I am. It is important for me to think that one day I want to emulate my boss. There is a balance between being very distant or very low-level. I expect my boss to be able to strike that balance.

ANSWER3: I have in the past worked for people who were not the best communicators. They were not clear about the details of the project or their own expectations so I know first-hand the effects of bad communication. These experiences have been good in a sense that I strive to be the opposite and make sure that I am clear about details and expectations.

❧

Have you ever made decisions without having all the information?

ANALYSIS: In some situations, the information will not be available to you or it will be hoarded from you. They are testing your ability to make sound judgment and to be a self-starter. Many roles are entrepreneurial in nature and you won't be spoon fed tasks especially as you move up the ladder.

ANSWER1: Ideally I would have all the information possible before embarking on a decision process. However in reality on most occasions, you have to make uninformed decisions. I draw on my experience, industry knowledge and solicit the expertise of my team to formulate decisions. I have given the go ahead to start the analysis on a production project without having secured the final mandate. Either way, we would learn something from it.

ANSWER2: One of the most important qualities of a leader is decisiveness. Team members and peers expect you to be able to make decisions as part of a vision. On occasion, you do have to make decisions without all the relevant information. You need to be able to make decisions that can adapt if more pertinent information comes along at a later stage. For example in my current role, I started recruiting for next year although our strategy was not finalized. We could redeploy the resources to other projects if we had to.

ANSWER3: I have a strong entrepreneurial spirit that will suit a small company like this. This industry is ever evolving and one of the key requirements for a person in this role will be the ability to make decisions so that the company can also evolve. Startups can take different directions as they evolve and that's what makes it so exciting. Your decisions may change but you should not be afraid to make measured ones in the first place. In the past, I have started branding products before the prototypes were fully completed. I know the process and the timescales to get this done and therefore know it is best to move ahead and you can tweak later.

How do you deal with multi-tasking projects?

ANALYSIS: Everyone needs to multi-task. Efficient multi-tasking is core to the workplace. They will have come across people who struggle with this and this will inhibit their career progression. Outline a few examples either that are internal or external to the office.

ANSWER1: In school, I was a member of the swim team, church gospel choir, I played lacrosse and ran the graduates welfare center. I had to juggle all this with my studies. I am well able to multi-task and I see that as a necessity for career progression.

ANSWER2: I wholly expect that I will have a number of tasks of varying complexity to perform at any one time as I always have in the past. I believe that it is important to manage your time to allow for efficient multi-tasking. I never understand anyone who wants to sit down and do the same thing all day every day. You will never grow that way.

ANSWER3: I have run virtual teams across different departments while still performing my daily tasks. I really enjoy having to multi-task as it is a great way to network, grow and learn more. Technological advancements have assisted us greatly in creating user groups and planning tools to take on additional work.

∽

How do you react when you are passed over for promotion?

ANALYSIS: Everyone at some stage will be disappointed with something that happens in the workplace. In many situations these disappointments center on pay and promotion. Sometimes, things won't go your way and indeed maybe unjust. You will be expected to be mature and accept these situations on occasion.

ANSWER1: Indeed I have and at the time it was disappointing for a brief moment. Instead of feeling hard done by, I looked at it as an opportunity to learn what I was missing and why my promotion was put on hold. I worked through some measurable goals with my boss and gained the promotion the year after.

ANSWER2: I was once and couldn't really figure out why. The only reason appeared to be that the other person was in the company a lot longer than me and they felt obliged to promote him. There really wasn't any defined promotion and feedback process. Therefore, I helped develop one so the situation was clear to all employees going forward.

ANSWER3: There is a flat structure where I work - no one has a title and therefore there are no promotions to speak of. In many ways, this does create a level playing field and we don't have people pulling rank on each another. However, some people are more progressive than others and should be recognized as so. Therefore, I am an advocate of the hierarchical recognition system that you have in place here.

෴

Have you ever become angry at work?

ANALYSIS: You probably have but that is not what they are concerned with. The question is why you got angry and were you un-professional? You can explain that any anger in the work place is a direct result of your passion for your work and out of respect for deadline and customer service. Sure, you may get frustrated from time to time but this has not been detrimental to your performance.

ANSWER1: Certainly not visibly! In the workplace, it is always best to keep one's composure even under times of stress. If people see you unravel, then it puts stress on everyone, creating a very negative and unproductive environment. If you do have an issue with someone, then discuss it with that person behind closed doors.

ANSWER2: I have certainly been annoyed by people not pulling their weight on occasion but have never allowed my temper to boil over. I don't believe that losing your head helps any situation inside or outside the office. I saw people do it on occasion and no good ever came of it.

ANSWER3: I was on the front line of customer service in my first job. It was part of our training as sales people to understand customer needs and indeed expectations. There were days when I felt like screaming as loud as I could but I always contained myself. I would have been fired if I lost my temper with a customer. It was a great training in retrospect.

ॐ

Do you have any record of indiscipline?

ANALYSIS: If you have a record of serious indiscipline such as fraud, theft or violence, it is likely to be found out at some stage. There are always two sides to the story and is better that she hears your side first. The last thing you want is to go through the whole process and a previous unmentioned indiscretion is brought to the attention of the company. It is better to pre-empt this.

ANSWER1: I don't, and my company takes a very dim view of any sort of indiscipline. Each case is always different and to be fair to all involved, any such cases should be investigated by someone with an objective viewpoint. In general, most cases are cut and dry but some accusations can stem from personal grievances.

ANSWER2: Our firm has been investigated on numerous occasions by the regulators. My boss and I had to brief the regulators at a special hearing. We were representing the company and were not being held personally or professionally liable. The case findings are public information and I can provide more information if required.

ANSWER3: The key to dealing with pressure is to remain calm and professional. Taking illegal or unprofessional short cuts may seem a necessity in the short-term but is never ever worth it in the long-term. You should never ethically compromise yourself or one of your colleagues.

What do you expect from a manager?

ANALYSIS: They are really asking what you expect from yourself, as she is looking to you to be a future manager. You should have very clear expectations of a manager's role and what is needed to succeed in management.

ANSWER1: I want to emulate my manager someday. I want to have his job when he moves on. In order to do this, I need to learn as much as I can from him or her. Managers need to inspire and motivate their staff. This creates great DNA that flows through a company.

ANSWER2: I expect my manager to have a succession plan for me. I have worked for people in the past who have had no intention of moving upwards as they were in a comfort zone. I found this very frustrating and this is one of the reasons that I have decided to move on.

ANSWER3: A manager should be a mentor for his/her staff. They need to guide, teach, praise and criticize when appropriate. In addition, a manager must look to hire people who are better than they are and give them the latitude to grow. Micro-management is not good for either the employee or the manager. A good manager can balance this.

ৎৎ

Why do you think you are a team player?

ANALYSIS: Of course you are! Any inference of the opposite will be absolutely catastrophic. Sure, everyone is expected to be self-motivated and a self-starter but you must always indicate that you can work within a team framework when called upon. Have some examples ready.

ANSWER1: On my year-end peer appraisals, I have always scored high on my team playing skills with peers, managers and fellow employees. I have worked hard to hone my team playing skills over the years as I learned at an early age that a cohesive team is a force to be reckoned with in the work place.

ANSWER2: I have been playing team sports since I could walk so team fabric is very familiar to me. Over the years, I was in many different positions in the sports teams ranging from captain to vice captain and on occasion omitted from the team. I have taken the team skills from the sports field to the office and applied them practically.

ANSWER3: I used to play a lot of tennis and chess. These are both great games and both require very individual and independent mindsets. When I first came to work, I struggled a bit with the team environment. I used my allocated training budget and some of my personal money to go on courses and workshops to learn about team playing. I found I really enjoyed them and have worked hard to become a great team player, as my colleagues will now attest to.

❧

What happens when someone says no to you?

ANALYSIS: They need to know that you are not pig headed and are able to negotiate professionally. Just like you will not agree with everyone, people won't always agree with you. You need to indicate that you are very capable of listening, taking on board a different point of view and reaching a compromise for the good of the business.

ANSWER1: People can always say no to me, in fact I actively encourage open dialog with all my colleagues. I don't profess to be a guru on everything but I am a very good listener. A core principal of team involvement is the ability to listen to and assess input from colleagues.

ANSWER2: Barking orders at people is not my style. If I am put in a leading position on a task that I am very familiar with, I will set out the process by which way things should be done. If someone has an issue with the procedure then they are more than welcome to voice their opinion and if the reasons are valid, I certainly will take them onboard.

ANSWER3: I think that it depends on the situation. In business, you sometimes have only a split second to make a decision and you have to follow your course of action. If someone disagrees with you, then it is going to be hard to change course. If it is someone you respect and trust, then you do need to carefully listen to his or her objections.

∽

When did you have to pull out the stops and go above your station?

ANALYSIS: They need to know that you can be depended upon to rise up when things are not going the way everyone wants it. Delayed projects, employee illness or employee departures are common occurrences. You need to be ready and armed to assist.

ANSWER1: I am very dependable and I will roll my sleeves up to get a job done. Flexibility is a very important part of teamwork. There will be times when things run late for various reasons and everyone is stretched. I have always taken this approach in my work and will continue to do so.

ANSWER2: Our office was hit really badly with a nasty flu. Seventy per cent of the workers were off ill. We were a small company so this was debilitating to our production. As team leader, I mandated that we all had to work extra hours for the sake of our customers. I led from the front and worked seven days a week at that time.

ANSWER3: In college, we had a case study to complete for submission as part as our final term examination. We discovered some new information that was contrary to the route we were taking only days before the deadline. I introduced a three-hour sleep rotation system for my partner and me to complete the study. It took us three days to complete and we had a huge sense of accomplishment when we finished.

What really irritates you in the work place?

ANALYSIS: It could be numerous things, from people to the work environment. They want to hear how you would change something that irritates you. Sometimes you can't change things that are out of your control but they do expect to hear some examples.

ANSWER1: Laziness really irritates me and I let my team know that is not acceptable. Any function or team is as only good as its weakest link. Each person has his or her skill and can add value in very different ways. I go out of my way to motivate people to exploit their existing skills and learn new ones.

ANSWER2: At times, I have found my management and immediate bosses' decisions surprising. Sometimes they are so detached from the day to day running of an operation, they make decisions based on perception rather than reality. This sometimes annoys me but instead of letting it get under my skin, I prefer to approach my seniors with a different solution that is more reflective of reality, keeping the end goals in mind. I feel that is best to be constructive in these situations.

ANSWER3: We depend heavily on our suppliers for parts to complete our production. We have six different components required and it is irritating when some suppliers are late with their delivery as it slows down our entire delivery process. I have learned to better estimate supplier delivery times and manage or eradicate those who are constantly late. This irritation has abated with experience.

∽

Do you have difficulties working with some people and why?

ANALYSIS: There are always people who are going to annoy you in the workplace. They are more interested in hearing how you resolve such issues and work with people you would not necessary choose to. The Interviewer expects to hear a positive answer here.

ANSWER1: In life, there are always going to be people I don't necessary see eye to eye with. I think that this is positive as it breeds constructive provocation and creativity. I tend to listen to everyone's point of view and if I am in fundamental disagreement, I explain why in a non-contentious manner. I find that this works best.

ANSWER2: I have come across people in the work place who have been difficult due to some insecurity or because they felt under threat with respect to their own ability. We come to work to get a job done for the sake of the company. If I have to take the moral high ground to surmount a difficult person, I will.

ANSWER3: I have learned not to take anything personally in the workplace. Some people are difficult for sometimes no apparent reason. They may have something else going on their lives. I work very well in a collaborative environment and refuse to be phased by difficult employees. You must keep pushing forwards for the sake of the team.

What kind of hours do you like to keep?

ANALYSIS: You need to demonstrate flexibility. You do not want to come across as a strict nine to five worker with a union mentality. Those who are willing to put in the extra hours are the ones who get ahead. They are looking for a future manager – act like one.

ANSWER1: I have a very flexible approach to working hours and I instill the same ethos in my team. At time, there will be a need to work fourteen hours a day to complete a project. I understand this and have no problem with it.

ANSWER2: Time management is a skill that everyone needs to learn in his or her career. When I began working, I was working every minute of every day. It was not necessarily more productive; it just meant that I had to manage my time better. I am much better at this but of course I remain flexible to working the extra hours when client demand merits it.

ANSWER3: For me, boredom is the worst form of stress. If I had a job where I was watching the clock all day, then I would simply be bored and should move on. I find that the days go by really quickly when I am challenged and on my feet all day long. Sometimes I am out at six other and times nine – I do what it takes to meet the goals and demands set for me.

೧൦

What sort of pressure have you been under in the workplace?

ANALYSIS: All work is pressure! You will have been under pressure for various reasons in and out of the workplace. They want to see how you coped with pressure, as this is something that you will be confronted with throughout your work life.

ANSWER1: Pressure is relative. Earlier in my career, I used to think that I was under a lot pressure. The fact was that I was in a new role and working full time was unfamiliar to me. As I grew older and advanced in my career, I began to feel less pressure and my productivity improved as a result.

ANSWER2: A work life balance is very important to reduce the pressure. I feel pressure sometimes when we are close to deadlines. The important thing I have learned is to relax and focus during the vital times in a project or production process. I make sure that I keep myself fit in body and mind to cope with this pressure.

ANSWER3: I absolutely revel in ambitious deadlines and demanding clients. I honestly believe that it brings out the best in me. A pressurized environment is not for everyone but I have no issues working in one.

∽

How loyal are you?

ANALYSIS: This is somewhat of a trick question, as you are either loyal or you are not. The interviewer wants to ensure that you have loyalty code for those whom you work for and work with.

ANSWER1: Loyalty to me is completely binary, you either are or you are not - no in between. I am loyal. There can't be any other way.

ANSWER2: I am completely loyal to the company I work for and to the people whom I work with. Loyalty is a foundation of trust. You need to trust and have the trust of the people you work with.

ANSWER3: Not being 100% loyal is not an option in the workplace. It is detrimental to project success and team building. Naturally loyalty does not include doing anything illegal or unprofessional.

 ∾

What is the biggest mistake you have made to date in the workplace?

ANALYSIS: Whatever the mistake was, they are more interested in what the resolution was and if the same mistake was repeated or not. You will make mistakes and there is no point pretending that you have not so ensure you have an example with the resolution.

ANSWER1: Yes, in my first week at my first job, I posted out the wrong statement to the wrong client. I admitted the mistake but my boss and client were livid and indeed he was on the brink of firing me. I was really disappointed with myself. I told my boss that he could fire me if it ever happened again. It never happened again and I learned a valuable lesson.

ANSWER2: I believe that everyone makes mistakes at work and that that is not necessary a bad thing. Everyone should learn from their own mistakes and those of others. I once misread how long a project would take and really messed up the planning stage. I learnt that I needed to be a bit more conservative and plan for the unknown; I have been pretty accurate since.

ANSWER3: My biggest mistake was to assume that an outside vendor would deliver a vital component to us on time as I had paid him upfront. After much chasing, the components were delivered three weeks late and push back our delivery to our irate client by five weeks in total. I learned never to pay someone upfront again and also learned how to better manage a client's expectation.

৶

Have you ever had a dispute with a boss?

ANALYSIS: It is possible you may have. They want to know if you have the ability to "agree to disagree" on occasion. It is not a crime to not agree with your boss on everything but there is a mode to articulate it. You should have some examples that had a positive outcome.

ANSWER1: I have always had a healthy and respectful relationship with my bosses. I am the kind of person who likes to let my boss know when I feel strongly that an approach should be taken in a different direction. I am not always right but the open dialog helps us to assess any potential problems and this ultimately benefits the task.

ANSWER2: One time I felt we could automate the second phase of production differently to accommodate surging demand. The firm had done it one way forever. My boss was slow to change but to his credit he listened to my step-by step approach and agreed. It worked well for all of us and I respect him for agreeing to make the change.

ANSWER3: I believe that every boss should be open to listening to his employees. This takes a certain level of maturity and some bosses still prefer a military type attitude to the workplace – their way or no way. If their way is the most efficient and effective then we should all agree, if not then I have felt honor bound to point this out in a constructive manner that has benefited the firm.

How do you deal with conflict?

ANALYSIS: Conflict resolution is a common occurrence in the workplace. You will be faced by this challenge throughout your career. You need to demonstrate that you are a good listener and possess the ability to resolve disputes that put deliverables at risk.

ANSWER1: I am a firm believer that everyone has a valid view. Usually at the beginning of a project, I will solicit everyone's viewpoint on the best way to proceed. It gives everyone a sense of ownership and promotes compromise. Above all, it lessens the probability of disagreement later on. This approach has worked well for me.

ANSWER2: Conflicts are not uncommon and can be exaggerated when timelines are being missed and consistently delayed. I never allow a conflict to fester to the detriment of the project. It is important to listen to all sides of the argument. I therefore look for a resolution that keeps the work on track without disenfranchising anyone.

ANSWER3: I have worked for ten years and dealt with much conflict that arose from pressure and stress. In all situations bar one, I managed to diffuse the conflicts by listening, assessing and providing a solution. In the one exceptional case, the employee had no interest in being a team player and consistently upset everyone else on the team and put the project in jeopardy. I had him relocated to a different project.

Can you adapt to someone else's mode of work?

ANALYSIS: Everyone has a unique approach to work, but it is important to accept the way other people work also. You will be expected to bring some fresh ideas but also must be respectful of the way work is conducted at the company currently. The interviewer will want to know how you strike a balance with this.

ANSWER1: No matter what age or rank you are, you should still be willing to learn. Every industry is still evolving and you need to adapt with it. I believe that work is a compromise and that every individual will bring certain uniqueness to the workplace.

ANSWER2: If the work is a more defined production process, then absolutely one should adapt to the policy implemented by predecessors for both safety and legal reasons. However, it is always ok to offer fresh suggestions on improvements. They may or may not be entertained but it shows motivation and commitment on your part.

ANSWER3: At a very junior level, it is important to adapt to your bosses style. At that time, everything is new to you and you should respect the experience of a senior. As you become more confident with the work and processes, you should be in a position to develop your own work style that people below you can adapt to.

၆

Have you ever been put on the spot?

ANALYSIS: At some stage in your life or work career, you will have been put in an awkward situation or asked a question that you may not know the answer to. They are more interested in how you dealt with the situation and how professional you were in handling it.

ANSWER1: A work colleague presented my work at a meeting as his own. It was a senior management meeting and the acknowledgment would have really increased my profile. I bit my tongue at the meeting as I felt it was best to remain professional. We discussed the situation later. I believe that during the course of your career, you will be put on the spot and in difficult positions from time. It is important to remain assertive but professional.

ANSWER2: A very difficult customer came bursting through the door unannounced one afternoon. He was demanding a refund for his products because of a perceived lack of quality. I was courteous but did not give into his demands. I promised him that I would review the situation immediately and offered him a discount on his next purchase for his inconvenience. In a customer facing business, you should expect such situations from time to time.

ANSWER3: I was on the junior football team at school. Late one evening, I received a call from the coach of the senior team. Some key players were missing and he wanted me to play the next day. I was both nervous and excited, as these guys were all two years older than me. During your career, you will be hit with some unexpected challenges that you will need to step up to.

৽

How good are you at delegating?

ANALYSIS: The ability to delegate is important. It keeps your staff busy and motivated. In addition it is also important for your own succession plan as you prepare to ascend through the ranks. Your management does not want you to be a bottleneck for any of the business and you must give your staff the latitude to grow. They will be looking for some concrete examples.

ANSWER1: You need to trust your employees. We had a very difficult client who wanted a product market report completed yesterday. The only way I could complete this was by delegating the competitor analysis and industry growth projections to my staff and it worked very well. It is important that people at an early stage in their careers have a sense of responsibility. It is the onus of the manager to delegate tasks to nurture this sense.

ANSWER2: I would not have managed to successfully lead the large production for the company without delegating carefully among the staff. I delegated the development, quality assurance, user testing and release to team members whilst retaining the project management myself. Delegation is an absolute must for efficiency, promotion and succession.

ANSWER3: I do not have anyone working for me but do have an appreciation for efficient delegation. My company is very adamant that every employee must review his boss at year-end. My boss is a great mentor and visionary. One thing I do point out in his reviews is the need to delegate more. With more delegation, I know I can learn more and progress upwards.

಄

Do you tend to aim too high?

ANALYSIS: There is no harm in aiming too high as long as you don't over stress yourself and your team. Also, you will need to ensure that you don't over promise to management and consistently under deliver. They want to ensure that you understand how to match people's expectations with you and your team's ability to deliver.

ANSWER1: I think you should always aim high but you need to be somewhat realistic as well. When I deal with clients, while I always assure them that their goals will be met, I at the same time like to set their expectations in terms of what will be delivered, the associated cost and the timelines

ANSWER2: I am very ambitious and do want to rise to the top. I work hard and remain focused. If you aim too low, you will end up even lower. Who knows what will happen in the future to this company or this industry. I believe that through hard work, patience and taking responsibility, you can and should aim high.

ANSWER3: In College, I studied hard to be the top of my class. I attained top three ranking right across the board. However, I managed to keep a very active social life and worked out four times a week. I think it is important to maintain a healthy balanced lifestyle to help you achieve high ambitions. Therefore, I don't believe that I aim too high because I know I can attain what I set myself.

∽

Give an example of when you used good judgment.

ANALYSIS: Good judgment includes the ability to make informed decisions. This comes with experience and there is an element of satisfaction when your judgment proves to be correct. They will be looking for examples where your good judgment resulted in a positive outcome.

ANSWER1: Good judgment is core to any business decision. I have built up a business from scratch. I started with a business plan, secured funding, created the product, marketed it and brought it to market. Naturally, I was very emotionally invested in it. It was my baby. I was approached to sell the company and although it was difficult for me to do, I exercised good judgment in that I recognized that I could bring the company no further so I sold it. The product is still on the market today.

ANSWER2: I like to get involved in recruiting new graduates. They are the next generation of our company and I take the process very seriously. There are many qualified candidates who on paper could all be beneficial to our company. Therefore, I have to use good judgment in choosing among them. Good judgment is a combination of industry experience, knowing your company, knowing your product and an ability to identify new team members.

ANSWER3: I was captain of the school basketball team and we reached the regional finals. I went to watch our competition play in their semi-final. I spotted a hole in their defense play. The strategy to exploit this hole would require the skills of a player who was not a first team regular for us. I made the decision to start with this player much to the annoyance of the regular player. The strategy worked. Sometimes good judgment requires tough decisions to get ahead; I expect to be faced with this throughout my career.

෨

Have you ever managed to change someone's opinion?

ANALYSIS: Negotiation is a key part of business. You must be able to negotiate with your juniors and with your seniors. They will be interested in how you win people over. Sometimes this can be very challenging and you may have to dig deep to execute on this.

ANSWER1: My boss wanted us to put together the monthly client report in the usual manner. The template was there, so it was convenient. Every month, the client asked for additional information. I really wanted to change it but my boss refused to budge. One night after work, I drafted a new template that contained all the same information as the original one and the additional requests. I kept the format similar. My boss really liked it and we implemented the change. I learned that it is possible to change someone's mind if you have a strong alternative solution.

ANSWER2: If people see that you are trying to help them and are objective, they will be open to changing their opinion. A team member resigned. She was going to a competitor. She outlined the new role and her responsibilities. She told me the issues she had with her current role. We went through each of the issues one by one and matched or bettered them. She changed her opinion of the company and stayed and with us.

ANSWER3: People sometimes have an opinion without having all the facts. One of our team members on the basketball team was thrown out of the team for being constantly late for practice with no concrete excuse. The team captain was adamant that he would never play for us again. I visited the team member and could see that his family circumstances were not conducive to him coming to practice at those times. He was too embarrassed to give us the reasons. I explained this to the captain and he changed the times to help him.

ᮍ

Have you ever changed your opinion?

ANALYSIS: Sure you have, but why? Had you not analyzed the problem properly the first time? Did new information come to light later in a process? They are interested not only in what drove the change but also what the repercussions were of you making the change. Was it worth it?

ANSWER1: I have and I think you need to be flexible to do so. I was steering a project in one direction when some additional information came in from our research team. The new information was going to put us on a different route but would speed up the production cycle. I had structured the project in such a way that if I had to change my opinion I could and did change course. In business, you can be hit very quickly with an issue previously unknown, you need to adapt and it is ok to change your opinion for the good of the task in hand.

ANSWER2: I was not convinced of an employee's performance during the year to the extent that I was going to put him on notice. In my mind, he had continuously underperformed on the tasks set by his line manager. The employee wanted one more chance to turn my opinion around. I put him on probation. Not only did he turn himself around but he became an out performer. A year later, I had a totally different opinion of his work. I think it is important to expect employees to perform constantly but also need to be open minded to change any perceptions you may have.

ANSWER3: Opinions like rules are there to be changed if there is a strong case to do so. In college, I had editorial rights on the campus news for my final semester. All students read the paper. During the student council elections, I shocked our readership by changing my opinion on a candidate who I had previously backed. That candidate had run a very nasty and individualistic campaign. I had previously been a strong supporter. I think it takes a strong character to change your opinion.

❦

What do you do if you fundamentally disagree with a company policy?

ANALYSIS: They are testing your loyalty to the company's way and trying to ascertain if you are a maverick and a potential troublesome employee. Of course professional ethics should always trump any policy and if an unwritten policy of a company expects otherwise, you are in your rights to disagree with it.

ANSWER1: I always read company policies before accepting an offer. Many people don't do this, as it is a tedious exercise! If there is something that I fundamentally disagree with, I will always seek clarification. Usually there is no problem and just the interpretation needs to be clarified.

ANSWER2: Above all, it is always most important to conduct business in a professional and ethical way. If someone presents an idea or a practice that does not fit the conduct I expect, I will of course question it. This has never happened to me yet as I understand that the vast majority of companies adhere to professional practice.

ANSWER3: These days, most large companies have the counsel of attorneys and compliance officers either internal or external to the company. They spend a lot of time interpreting and clarifying regulation and issue statements on professional codes for employees. I would never break one of these. I may on occasion seek clarification but that has only happened twice in ten years.

❧

Have you ever had a personal conflict with a colleague?

ANALYSIS: They want to see what your professional ethics are and if you allow personal views get in the way of business. You may not like everyone you work or interact with. You may never want to see them outside of the workplace. However, while you are in the work place, you need to get on.

ANSWER1: No, I have never had any conflict like this in the work place. As a rule, I don't discuss personal views on topics such as religion, sexual orientation or even politics in the work place. I think there is a time and place for such discussion and when at work it is best to focus on the tasks at hand.

ANSWER2: I don't necessary have a personal relationship with all my colleagues in the sense that I am hanging out with them watching football on a Saturday. However, we all work together and share the vision and goals to be as productive as possible.

ANSWER3: We are a small company and we spend many hours together as we are in startup mode. We sometimes eat three meals a day together in order to get things done. Sometimes personal views on topics such as sports and politics arise, however, we all have mutual respect for each other and we don't allow personal views to morph into a conflict.

෴

What do you do with confidential information?

ANALYSIS: Confidential information is confidential for a reason and needs to be treated as such. You will need to indicate that there is no middle ground here. Any leak of confidential information is instant dismissal in the majority of cases. Confidential information ranges from Intellectual Property to accounts to client data to employee details.

ANSWER1: The only thing you can do with confidential information is to keep it confidential. In my last role, I worked very closely with our legal team to keep our intellectual property confidential. We patented all our new products to protect ourselves. Any leakage would have been detrimental to our business.

ANSWER2: Our clients are our business. I have heard of people selling client lists to other marketers for some short-term gain. We don't do this, as we believe that this is a breach of client confidence. We take all confidential issues very seriously and that is something that I have instilled in all my employees. If a client finds out that you have been shopping their information, he will not be your client for much longer.

ANSWER3: I have a huge circle of friends and I am a very close confident to all of them. If someone tells me something in confidence, it remains confident, period. Friends and colleagues need to know they can trust you. If you get a reputation for not being trustworthy, your colleagues will always be suspicious and that will impede your career progress.

༄

Have you ever had to adapt to a culturally different environment?

ANALYSIS: We live in an ever-evolving multi-cultural society. Technology has made the world a smaller place and has opened up avenues and culture that were previously inaccessible. They will need to know that you have a healthy understanding of diversity and do your best to integrate such values into your team and company where appropriate.

ANSWER1: I love the diversity of our industry. On any one day, I could be talking with someone from Australia to Austria. Communication advancements have opened up a world of opportunity from cross regional marketing to the outsourcing of technology. This is the way forward and people need to embrace it.

ANSWER2: I am from a very small town and as a student I worked at the local mall. Everyone was from the same town, practiced the same religion, same values and thought process. This worked fine as all our customers were of a similar background. However, I really feel that diversity would have encouraged creativity and therefore created new opportunities. When I moved to London, I really understood the value of diversity in the workplace.

ANSWER3: Appreciation and respect for diversity is core to any firm's ethos regardless of how large the company is or where it is located. Not having respect for a colleague's culture or beliefs is simply not having respect for that colleague. Teamwork is about respect for your colleagues, if you don't have that then the team fabric breaks and subsequently hurts the company. I embrace my colleague's beliefs and enjoy the benefits of working in a diverse culture.

༚

What is the best way to react in a work crisis?

ANALYSIS: A crisis can mean many things. It could be mean a final letter from your most important client, a factory explosion, a mass exodus of employees to a competitor or a deadly flu virus. They want to know you deal with unforeseen situations, what is your strategy and what you learn from them should they strike again.

ANSWER1: There are always going to be critical situations that arise in the workplace. Issues can range from late delivery, client disgruntlement to customer and employee dissatisfaction. It is always important to have a cool head. If you lose your temper, you could put your judgment and your business at risk by alienating people. For example, rumors emanating from outside the company suggested that we were about to be bought and broken up. These were untrue but the staff was very concerned. I called all my staff into my office, looked at them straight in the eye and told them that it was untrue. Effective communication can solve many perceived critical issues.

ANSWER2: Every critical situation requires strong leadership. Unfortunately, a member of our team died in a traffic accident. We were all distraught. As team leader, I had to break the news to the staff. I ensured that the situation was handled very delicately. I arranged for professional counselors to be onsite to help the staff and let people take the time they needed to grief. People always need a leader in these situations and I fulfilled that role.

ANSWER3: Every situation is unique and needs to be diffused differently. A client was threatening to move his business to another firm; it was a huge account, our largest in fact. I listened intently to the client's issues with us and worked out a compromise that was appealing to him. It is best to avert a crisis as early as you can. I believe that there is a solution available to every crisis once you break it down and get to nucleus of the issue.

∽

How rigid do you stick to your goals?

ANALYSIS: They want to know that you can balance strict deadlines with a level of flexibility if necessary. Things change in the workplace all the time. This could be driven by internal factors such as management shakeup or by external factors such as regulation or competitive forces. Always be willing to embrace change.

ANSWER1: It is important to set goals and stick to them. Everyone in the workplace needs some structure. I like to set mini goals each day - inside and outside the office. Naturally, the goals should be attainable and formulated to aim for a larger goal. Achieving the daily goals gives me a sense of accomplishment.

ANSWER2: There is nothing better than setting goals and achieving them. I stick to the goals as rigidly as I possibly can. Sometimes, the original goals have to be reviewed or reset. This usually happens when a production, a project or a client deadline changes. You have to adapt to such change.

ANSWER3: My goals are my team's and client's goals. Therefore I take goal setting very seriously. This is a discipline that I instill in all my staff. If your personal goals are not in line with the client and the rest of the team, then there is an issue. What is right for the firm is good for the employee.

◌◞◌

What happens if you miss your goals?

ANALYSIS: There will be times when you miss goals that have been set by you or by your management. Missing the goal is not the issue but more how you communicate missing the goal and how you managed the expectations of the customer, management, team and yourself.

ANSWER1: Goals change over time and in fact evolve as one matures. This happens throughout life and not just in the workplace. I like to keep my more strict goals short-term and attainable. These are harder to miss. If there are missed then I have become better at understanding why. I have long-term high -level goals also.

ANSWER2: Goals need to be constantly reviewed. Many people don't realize that achieving goals is an iterative process. The goals need to be measurable and achievable. When I mentor junior employees, I always urge this approach. Any goals that are missed are then fully assessed as to what we can do better the next time.

ANSWER3: I am disappointed with myself if I fail to hit a goal. I take goal achievement very seriously and put pressure on myself to hit the right levels. The reasons for not achieving goals vary from milestones being too aggressive to external factors. The times I have missed goals has dramatically decreased over the years and are now not really an issue.

༄

Has your work ever been criticized by peers?

ANALYSIS: If you say no, the interviewers will not and should not believe you. They want to know how you respond to criticism and how professional you are in such circumstances. You should indicate the positives of teamwork and peer appraisal that has helped you grow and mature in your career to date.

ANSWER1: Yes, I have and at the time I did think it was unfair and biased. However, on reflection later, I was more objective in my analysis and felt that there was some truth in what they were saying. I learned from it and worked on the issue in question and have not heard such criticisms since. In fact, the biggest lesson learned was that sometimes criticism is constructive. You need to remain open-minded and depersonalize the criticism.

ANSWER2: I believe that criticism is good for you. People can criticize you for various reasons, some of it very constructive, others more because they are threatened by you. I feel it is important to listen to consensus critique and do not take it to heart because if you turn the situation around, it will help you even more.

ANSWER3: I do not think that I would have reached my current position without receiving some criticism. Anytime

I am criticized for whatever reason, I use it as reason to either learn more about the person who is criticizing me and about myself. I truly believe that peer reviews are key to a successful team and business.

∽

How do you deal with irate customers?

ANALYSIS: Customers can be irate for many reasons and indeed some of them unreasonable. In some industries, more than others, you are going to be faced with this every day. They want to know how you cope in these situations. You may not like it, but if they are asking you this, they are implying that this is going to be something that the role demands. Have some positive examples ready.

ANSWER1: Customers or clients can be very demanding and therefore very frustrating. However, in many cases, they are justified and their expectations simply have not been managed or met. I like to engage with my customers very frequently and I am not afraid to deliver bad news if I have to. If the customer has been engaged, they rarely become too unreasonable as their expectations are met.

ANSWER2: In ninety nine percent of cases, customers are angry because you have not delivered or met their expectations. Honesty and integrity is the best way to deal with an irate customer, understand it from their point of view and learn from it so that won't happen again.

ANSWER3: Overpromising and under delivering is something that affects us all, inside and outside the work place. If business is booming, then make sure you are staffed correctly because if not, you will compromise your business. Customers have long memories and when the economy becomes quiet again, they will remember how you treated them when things were good for you. Customer loyalty is a priority for any business.

CHAPTER 5: SALARY EXPECTATION, RELOCATION AND RESIGNATION

Introduction

This is a tricky interview area and questions here are hard to answer. It depends on what stage of the process you are at and questions like these can be a bit of game during the early stages.

Your research should give you an indication of what is fair for your rank in your industry. Give a range without over committing or selling yourself short.

They will want to know if you are going to find it difficult to leave your current job and how serious you are about this job. Be prepared for questions on relocation and travel also.

ॐ

What are your salary expectations?

ANALYSIS: Before you go to the interview, you should have a fair idea what is on offer via research. They are going to know your previous salary so it is always best to give a range starting from your current to a higher level. Don't be unrealistic but be aggressive.

ANSWER1: I believe that my range is in line with the industry standard for someone with my experience, rank and ambition. Your company has a very good reputation for being fair with compensation so should you make me an offer; I don't think we will have an issue.

ANSWER2: I know that I can make a big difference here so I expect that the compensation package will reflect that potential. I find that salary negotiation is only one component in the process. Should an offer be made, then we can consider a number of factors and view the package on the whole rather than just salary alone.

ANSWER3: When the recruiter contacted me about this role, she gave me a range that I believe was fair in terms of my expectations. Future and potential earnings are as important to me as current compensation. Your company offers career growth that is really attractive to me.

☙

We can't pay you the kind of money you have been earning – are you willing to take a pay cut?

ANALYSIS: This depends on the role and the how different your new company is in comparison to your old one. If you know you are moving into a space that will pay less than your previous salary, you may be in a position to accept less in lieu of some real responsibility and career growth.

ANSWER1: I look to the long term. The ability to grow in a role and have a career path to senior management is very important to me. I am willing to be creative with the compensation package in lieu of this. I assume that senior positions will be compensated accordingly.

ANSWER2: I understand that the compensation model on this side of industry is not as highly paid as the side that I am currently on. I want to make the change as I feel it is the right time in my career to do this. I am willing to be paid in line with what someone with my experience would expect in this area.

ANSWER3: This Company is in the same sector and side of the industry as my current company. I am not expecting any sign-on bonuses or incentives but would look for a fair market rate for someone with my experience and rank. Each company has its own structure and I am open to a creative solution if my current package is deemed too high.

രൂ

How come you have not earned as much as you should have?

ANALYSIS: They are looking for your reaction to this. You can turn it around as one of the reasons that you are now looking to leave.

ANSWER1: I believe that this is a function of the industry that I am in and the companies that I have worked for. I don't believe that I was paid less than others at my level and comparative responsibility within the company.

ANSWER2: I always realized that in comparison to peers at other firms, I have been slightly underpaid. The reasons I stayed put were due to the fact that I was still challenged and learning a lot about the business and I felt that this outweighed the monetary gain at that stage of my career.

ANSWER3: My current job is my first from school and therefore I never really questioned how much I should be making. I needed experience in this field and this company provided it to me. It is a small family company and doesn't have any ambitions to grow further. I expect that based on my experience I will get paid more for a role at another company.

෬෧

Are you expecting deferred compensation and/or share options from your previous firm to be paid?

ANALYSIS: If you have a substantial amount of deferred compensation at your existing company and are moving to a company that does not have a similar scheme, this can be a tricky question. You don't want this to be a deal breaker so it is best to keep your answer vague and say that you are open to alternatives.

ANSWER1: At my current company, deferred compensation formed approximately thirty per cent of my pay each year which was then spread out over three years. I do have a substantial amount and I view it as money earned and therefore owed to me. I am aware that you have a similar set up here and assume that this would be factored into any offer.

ANSWER2: I do have some cash deferred compensation at my current company that I have accumulated over the past few years. I know that you do not have this practice so I am open to a creative solution should you make me a job offer.

ANSWER3: I have some share options that are in the money but I am not allowed to exercise them before their expiry date that is in six months. If you have a similar employee profit sharing scheme, it would be good to be able to transfer these into your scheme in a fair value way.

෨

Will you take shares or options in lieu of cash?

ANALYSIS: This depends on the company you are going to and what your own financial situation is. They want to know how flexible you are and how much you really want this job.

The fact that they are asking the question suggests that there is a strong employee ownership policy at this firm.

ANSWER1: This is a start up venture and therefore I understand that share options and shares are probably going to be the primary mode of compensation. I really believe in the business plan, the product and the niche you are entering. Therefore I am prepared to take the risk with you.

ANSWER2: I am open to a creative compensation package. As I have a young family, there will be a minimum cash component that I will need in order to survive. I truly believe that I will be able to immediately implement change for you through this role and expect that in the long term, I will be compensated accordingly should the company's revenues grow as expected.

ANSWER3: Naturally, the devil is in the details but on the surface of it, a combination package is acceptable. I would not always opt for this with most companies but the reputation of this company in terms of its professionalism and balance sheet is second to none.

ᖶ

We cannot offer you a full comprehensive benefits package as we are too small –are you ok with that?

ANALYSIS: You may not be. They want to see if this is a surprise to you or not. You should give the indication that you are open to flexible arrangements and try to leave such discussions until you are in the final negotiation phase with the new company.

ANSWER1: I was unaware of this and appreciate that you are being up front about this. My wife is a stay at home mom so I will need to take this into account in terms the total compensation should an offer be made. I really would love to join here and so will see if I can make something work.

ANSWER2: Naturally as this is a startup, I don't expect a competitive package in terms of the cash component. I really believe in what you want to do here so I am sure we can work something out.

ANSWER3: Having no benefits would be quite difficult for my family and me. If there are other creative ways to compensate for this, I would be open to discussion. But having zero medical benefits would be difficult.

෴

Are you leaving your current role for monetary reasons?

ANALYSIS: They want to understand your true motivation for leaving. If it really is money, you will need to downplay it and sell the interviewer on the idea that you want career growth and opportunity. You will expect the money to come with that if you flourish as expected at the new company.

ANSWER1: No, not at all. The company has treated me well over the past few years. My main motivation for leaving is I believe that I have hit the proverbial glass ceiling. I cannot see a career path to satisfy my ambitions. My role there has reached a plateau and I need a fresh challenge.

ANSWER2: I believe that if you have career growth and opportunity then the money will come. The company I am with is struggling and has cut back both its production and R &D. My role is safe there but it is essentially in maintenance mode. I am looking for a new career opportunity.

ANSWER3: I have consistently achieved top grades in my year-end reviews both from peers and management. The company is about to be sold and I am quite sure that the culture will change substantially. I know that your company has a similar work ethos to the one I am in so I think this would be a great move for me.

೧৩

You have been with your company a long time – why switch now?

ANALYSIS: You will have to be very clear on your motives for wanting to leave. You may feel that you have reached the end of your career there. There may be politics involved. Do not to overly criticize your current company because the interviewer will not be impressed.

ANSWER1: I don't think that there is ever a good or bad time to leave a company. I have stayed where I am because I have had very positive experiences in terms of growth and career prospects. The company wants to secure its captive client base and doesn't want to expand anymore. I love the challenge of companies that want to keep evolving such as yours.

ANSWER2: I am one of the co-founders of the company. Over the past five years, I have seen us grow from a two to twenty person team. It is public information that we have entered an agreement to sell the company and the horizontal integration to the new company means that there won't be a spot for me. I am excited about bringing my skills to another growing company such as yours.

ANSWER3: I have thought the next move through very carefully for quite some time now. Naturally, it is always different when you are at my stage of your career to make a change. But I am a firm believer in personal and career growth. This role and your company is one of the few places that provide me with this combination at this point.

℘

Will you find it difficult to leave your current company?

ANALYSIS: You probably will, especially if you have consolidated your position. They really need to know that you are committed to leaving and not trying to "play" your current company into giving you a counter-offer to further your career. They really do not want to waste their own or their colleague's time interviewing you for no reason.

ANSWER1: Yes, I have been with the company for more than ten years now and have built up a very strong network internally. I have thought long and hard about the next move. I believe that I have hit a glass ceiling there and it is time for the next challenge. Therefore I will not have any issues with resigning at this time.

ANSWER2: My current company cannot offer me the growth that I aspire to. I have been looking for the next move internally for some time now and there does not appear to be an avenue for me. I am looking for my next big career move and I believe that this role and company can satisfy those needs.

ANSWER3: Leaving a company after such a long time can be difficult. The benefit of being there such a long time is that I am very in tune with the strategic direction and where my career could go. I could stay and be very comfortable but I need to be continuously challenged and that is why I am looking to leave. I am very comfortable with my decision to leave now.

∽

You will be required to travel 25% of the time – is that an issue?

ANALYSIS: You should be aware of this before going into the interview, so if you act surprised, that could annoy them. You should say that this is not a problem. They are obliged to let you know that there is some travelling involved and it may not be as much as 25%.

ANSWER1: Travelling does not bother me at all. It is always good to meet clients and team members in other regions. This is a global product and therefore merits input from all relevant areas of the globe. It also gives me an opportunity to evolve the business in disparate regions in tandem.

ANSWER2: I used to work for a large multi-national. My location and office was very much on the periphery of the business. We never really got a say in the direction of the product or the business and the disengagement led to disgruntlement. I am acutely aware of the importance of travelling and engaging employees in all locations.

ANSWER3: Given the nature of the business, I am not surprised that there is extensive travelling required. My research indicates that for the business model to be successful there is a two-year window to brand and market the product nationwide. Therefore, I see travelling as core to this function and don't have any issue with that at all

ᕤᕥ

Are you will to relocate?

ANALYSIS: The chances are that you should be expecting this. If you are applying for a job in Boston and live in New York currently, you will have to re-locate. Also, as the role evolves, you may be requested to relocate overseas. Remain flexible and open to any suggestions at this stage.

ANSWER1: I have already discussed this with my family and we are willing to relocate. We see this as a great opportunity for me and the upheaval would be minimal. Our kids are young and are at an age where a school change would be exciting for them.

ANSWER2: I have always wanted to work in another country and should that opportunity present itself within this role, I would have no hesitation in put my name forward to re-locate. I believe that you will get a more rounded experience working in different countries and diverse cultures.

ANSWER3: I was fully aware of the location of the role before I applied for the role so relocation will not be an issue for me. Indeed, I am also open to any further re-location as the role evolves.

CHAPTER 6: YOUR EDUCATION

Introduction

If this is your first job interview, then prepare for many questions. The further you are along in your career, the fewer questions you will be asked on this subject. On many occasions, you will end up doing something different than what you studied. The interviewer will want to know that you have appreciated the value of an education and the benefits

What would you change about your college?

ANALYSIS: You may love your college and think it is a perfect place, which is great! However, one of the key characteristics recruiters look for is the ability to suggest and implement change. You will need to impress on them that you have a number of ideas and know how they could be implemented.

ANSWER1: I really loved my college, the atmosphere is friendly and the people are relaxed but motivated. There is however always room for improvement. I would prefer to see more practical and real world case studies in the business courses to prepare people for work life. Some of the business courses are very theoretical.

ANSWER2: The College has a fantastic academic reputation, constantly scoring in the top 20 on a number of academic levels. However, it needs to expand its extra-curricular activities. One of the reasons that this is not at the highest level is that the college has a very weak endowment program. They should look to their well-educated graduates for help with this. I would like to help with this.

ANSWER3: I am very grateful that I had the opportunity to go this great college and in many ways I think it was perfect. I would implement a senior to junior student mentoring program across all the faculties. This would be a great help to the junior students in choosing subjects, learning how to approach prospective employers and avoid any potential pitfalls that seniors may have made.

Are grades in reality an indication that you will do well in the workplace?

ANALYSIS: This somewhat dependant on your own grades and position in the class. Having great grades will indicate that you are smart, disciplined, self-motivated, can independently research and are determined. Bad grades may indicate that you have channeled your energies elsewhere, have chosen the wrong course or may have personal issues.

ANSWER1: Although I do have very good grades and have constantly ranked at the top of my class, I feel that the extracurricular activities that I was involved in have helped round my character. I find that it is as just as important to build a network as it is to rank top of the class.

ANSWER2: As you can see my grades were mid ranking. However, this did not impede my progress in the workplace. I am hungry, self-motivated and ambitious. These are the ingredients you need to succeed. I was very active in a number of societies in college and this did take some focus from my studies. However, I believe that multi-tasking prepared me more for the workplace. There are plenty of people who work for me now who have grades much higher than me.

ANSWER3: Good grades are certainly symptomatic of someone who has discipline and a willingness to work hard on their own. But you do need to be able to channel this into teamwork in your career. Many academically brilliant people do fail in the work place because the environment is not as individualistic as school and study can be.

∾

Why have you not considered a postgraduate degree?

ANALYSIS: She wants to know that you are really committed working in the short to medium term. There may be an opportunity to do a business related course at a later stage. She wants to know that you really want the job and if you are somewhat undecided, there will be a peer happy enough to snap it up.

ANSWER1: I felt that I was ready for the workplace as soon as my undergraduate degree was completed. I had worked as an intern through my summers and had learned enough to see that progressing my studies further would not give me an edge in this industry where you need to learn on the job.

ANSWER2: My professor wanted me to pursue a doctorate. He felt that I should not sell my soul to banking! However, I simply did not want to become an academic and felt that if your heart is not in something, it makes it very hard to pursue. I am really looking forwards to getting into the industry and applying theory to practice. I believe that a higher degree would be too theoretical and not add further value to this role.

ANSWER3: An MBA would be interesting at some stage, maybe in five years or so. I really believe that to extract the maximum benefit from such a program, you do have to work for a number of years. I know that your company does sponsor part-time programs and this is something that I would be interested in after a few years.

๑๏

Was that the school of your choice?

ANALYSIS: They are really not that interested in knocking your school but want to see your reaction to the question. In particular if it wasn't, they want to know that you are still positive about your experiences there and what you have learned to bring to your work life.

ANSWER1: It was always my first choice. I worked hard to get there and was not disappointed when I got there. The balance between hard work and social life has stood me in good stealth in my work career and will continue to do so.

ANSWER2: Actually it wasn't and I was very disappointed at first. However, I learned a valuable lesson at an early stage about looking forward. Once I set foot in that school, I got immersed in college life both from a social and study point of view. It was the best experience I ever had.

ANSWER3: I couldn't decide between school A and B for a very long time. Finally I chose B. I learned that when you make such a big decision, you need to work at ensuring that it is the right decision and should not dwell on what could have been if I had taken the other option.

๑๏

How do you rate the program there as against other schools?

ANALYSIS: If it is the best course in the country or even not the best, she doesn't really need to hear you knocking other schools. They are seeing how professional you are and diplomatic when comparing schools. You will need diplomatic skills in any workplace.

ANSWER1: My school has been consistently ranked in the top 20 for the past ten years and the program was one of its signature courses. The competition was intense but healthy and helped extract the best from everyone. I made many friends who now also work in this industry.

ANSWER2: The program was as good as anywhere else. The main benefit of the program was that it was very focused on collaborative teamwork. We studied and researched in groups and the team structure is very similar to that practiced in the workplace. This has been very valuable in my career.

ANSWER3: I went to a small little known school. The close confines of the campus meant that everyone had to interact a lot both socially and in the classroom. I manage to build up a very strong network and a strong appreciation for teamwork

ᘒ

What did you learn that is relevant?

ANALYSIS: The truth could be absolutely nothing! You could be interviewing for an accountancy role as a chemical engineering major. They expect you to discuss course discipline, social interaction and how you approach work. Note not everything you do at work will be always interesting and sometimes relevant.

ANSWER1: I have a fine arts degree and work as an accountant so on the surface it does look like school was totally irrelevant. I would argue that any form of education is relevant. The discipline of research and study are important ingredients in any work life.

ANSWER2: I studied computer science and I have been programming since, so it is very relevant for me in that respect. However, I learned a lot more in school beyond the content of my course. I had to motivate myself to study, adhere to deadlines and work as a part of a team to complete fieldwork. The latter has really helped me in my career.

ANSWER3: The content of the coursework was pretty irrelevant in my particular case. I really learned a lot about people and diversity. I was a member of many clubs and societies and worked to raise funds for numerous good causes. The collaboration and teamwork were among the best learning experiences of my life to date.

∞

How did your experience in school prepare you for business life?

ANALYSIS: This could be either academic or something within a college society or a mixture of both. What they really want to know is if you can match some real life experience to the workplace. Situations arise in schools that are similar in terms of definition, conflict and resolution to those in the workplace.

ANSWER1: I was the bursar for the debating society at school. My role was to seek sponsorship, collect funds and plan for the year ahead. We travelled around the country a lot and entered many competitions. I had to budget for all these. It gave me a great insight into putting together a strategy a budget and executing it all.

ANSWER2: I was team captain for the school swimming team. We had eight individual and relay team spots. Two guys were neck and neck for the two hundred meter freestyle - I had to choose one. I felt that one had consistently trained harder and was more of a team player in terms of motivation for others. I chose him. I gave my reasons to the other who was very upset. I know that I will be faced with such situations in the workplace.

ANSWER3: I always thought that I had no interest in computing. During a business module, we were given a 101 on spreadsheets. I was amazed by the power of the functionality and how you could simplify some very complex processes. I took an additional module outside the course curriculum to learn more. I use spreadsheets as one of my main tools in the workplace.

❧

What is your ideal job after graduation?

ANALYSIS: This question is obviously directed at students. You may not be one hundred per cent sure at this stage, but something made you fill out this application form. Ask yourself what that was. They want to know that something in this industry as tweaked your interest - what is it and why?

ANSWER1: I have always wanted to work in this industry as a business analyst. I have closely followed the changes in regulation and find the dynamic pace of the environment fascinating. I have carefully chosen my college courses to prepare me for such a role.

ANSWER2: I was in two minds about pursuing a research role or a production role. Your presentation to our class a few nights ago and the subsequent Q & A really helped set my mind straight. I believe that research is the ideal role for me and that my ability to self-motivate, my grades and my course work all point in that direction.

ANSWER3: I want to gain as much experience as possible and expose myself to a number of roles. I am very entrepreneurial by nature, as is evident from my resume. A startup company like this offers the most interesting prospect for someone like me. I want to immerse themselves in all facets of the business from design, creation, production and branding.

CHAPTER 7: CAREER BREAKS, OTHER PROSPECTS AND NUMBER OF PAST JOBS

Introduction

If you have jumped from job to job quite frequently, this may raise an alarm bell with the interviewer. Make sure that you are prepared, as they will not ask straight out.

Likewise if you have taken a number of career breaks, please ensure that any hole in your resume is accounted for. The reasons can range from personal reasons, to being laid off or to just wanting a break.

They will expect that you are looking at other opportunities if you are serious about making a move. Make sure that your searches don't appear too different from the role you are interviewing for!

☙

There is a long gap on your resume – what were you doing during that period?

ANALYSIS: You need to ensure that you have omitted nothing on your resume either by mistake or deliberately. This will raise alarm bells. Ensure that all your time is accounted for.

ANSWER1: In between my first and second job, I travelled the world, visiting over thirty countries along the way. I found it a fantastic experience, meeting people from so many diverse cultures. The whole trip was a project in itself with a plan, a budget and plenty of risk mitigations at different stages.

ANSWER2: I was seriously injured in a car crash a number of years. I had to go undergo numerous surgeries and was confined to bed and the sofa for a year. I could not work during this period. Instead of watching TV all day and feeling sorry for myself, I thought myself how to program on the Internet and set up a cottage business of creating websites for friends and family.

ANSWER3: Unfortunately, my father passed very suddenly a few years ago and my other siblings had a hard time coping with managing the family affairs. I decided to take a career break at that time and took control of the situation. I gained some very valuable experience dealing with accountants, lawyers and bankers!

Do you intend taking another break?

ANALYSIS: They want to understand if this is just a short-term solution for you – maybe to raise some additional money to take another break. The nature of the role will dictate how important this is (you may be applying for seasonal work so it is fully acceptable that you will be taking another break). In general, your intention should be to stay with the company.

ANSWER1: No, I want to completely focus on my career now. I do believe that the break did me good and was fortunate to have gained unexpected valuable project management experience. This role and the career path merit full focus for the next ten years.

ANSWER2: I see this role as a fantastic opportunity and always something I want to do. You have explained the career path that goes with this role. I really want to throw my energy into growing my career and opportunities like these do not come up that often. A career break would not be on the horizon for me.

ANSWER3: My previous break was to tour the world, it was something I always wanted to do and now it is out of my system. My career is now my full focus. I have very valuable experience that I can bring to this role and the opportunity is really unique and exciting.

৵

You have been out of work for a while –what have you being doing?

ANALYSIS: There always is a reason for being out of work for a while be it by choice or not. They really want to know how you filled your days. Was it spent in front of the TV or in the local bar watching sports games? Project the image that you kept a structured lifestyle and filled your days whilst in pursuit of the next opportunity.

ANSWER1: My next move is very important to me so I have been taking the time to speak to as many people as possible in the industry with respect to what the best step for me is. I have joined online business networking communities and have made a number of new contacts. Many have pointed to your company and as soon as this role opened up, I applied for it.

ANSWER2: The restructuring at my last company happened at the beginning of the summer. There was not any real activity in the hiring front over the summer months. I used the time constructively to research potential opportunities and to keep abreast of industry developments. I am aware of the new regulations that are currently going through Congress and I am up to speed on every new product and process on the market.

ANSWER3: I have been doing some small ad hoc consultancy work to pay the bills. The consultancy work ensures that I am still very much in tune with what is going on in the industry. In addition, it has opened my eyes to opportunities to take my career in a potentially different direction. I can now see that many skills can be applied in numerous areas. This is why I was prompted to apply for this position.

℘

What criteria are you using to select companies to interview with?

ANALYSIS: The interviewers expect that you will be applying for similar roles in other companies within the industry. They expect that you have exercised some judgment when applying to these companies. So when you say something like you only want to work in a startup - are you being consistent?

ANSWER1: I have researched this industry thoroughly and have made a short list of the top companies. My criteria are opportunity, career growth, ambition and vision. I believe that this role in a market leading company such as yours would be a fantastic career growing opportunity.

ANSWER2: I want to work for a small ambitious company that is not afraid to take risks. I have worked for many years in big corporations. That was a great learning experience but now I want to have a greater sense of ownership and responsibility. Therefore I am applying to smaller companies only.

ANSWER3: I like companies with a social conscience. You have a great track record with green initiatives and a dedication to community affairs. This coupled with your well-publicized five-year growth plan were deciding factors for me.

℘

You have been at many different companies in a short period of time?

ANALYSIS: You may have been on contract work and are now applying for a permanent position. You will need to be clear on the change of work mode and why you want to be a permanent employee. You may have moved around in permanent positions voluntarily or involuntarily. In either case, you will need to sell them on the fact that there has been similarity and connections between the previous roles culminating in a natural evolution to this role.

ANSWER1: To date all my roles have been contracting. A long-term permanent position was not on offer for the type of work I do. Although, I was independent contractor, I did get to lead teams of full time employees and other contractors. The permanent nature of this role is an additional appeal for me.

ANSWER2: I have moved around a few times but there has been an underlying step up with each role. I was quite junior at the first role and the second one was a promotion for me. The third role again built on my skill set and allowed me to expand to the point where I could apply for the job at your company. I believe that it is important to keep building one's skill set. Ideally, I would like to do this at one company.

ANSWER3: One of the main reasons for applying for this role is because I see a long-term career for myself here. I have moved around in the past, as the roles were either oversold to me or too narrow in focus to allow me to grow further. Career progression is very important to me so I am excited about the prospect of working here.

∾

Are you interviewing elsewhere?

ANALYSIS: It is perfectly acceptable to be interviewing at other companies. However, ensure that they are similar roles to what you are currently interviewing for. If it is something quite different, then that will put your intentions for this career path into question.

ANSWER1: Yes, I am at some early stage discussions with two of your competitors. The roles there are similar but this role is the most interesting for me in terms of challenge and career growth. I have really enjoyed the people I have met here and their enthusiasm is compelling.

ANSWER2: I do have an offer from another company. I have not accepted it as I wanted to complete the process with your company. Your company is much further along in terms of its product, innovation and commitment to employee satisfaction. Should you make me an offer; it would be an easy choice for me to join here.

ANSWER3: You are the first company that I have applied to. My current situation is not disastrous and I always promised myself that I would only apply for something if it really caught my attention. The role on offer here is very unique and creative. I see this as a once in a lifetime opportunity.

∾

What are your timescales?

ANALYSIS: If you have vacation planned or if you are going to be held to "gardening leave" by your current company, it is best to be up front about it. They ideally may like you start as soon as possible but will understand that there may be reasons you can't. If you are the right candidate, they will wait for you.

ANSWER1: I do have a month's notice period from the time I resign. I would like to start immediately thereafter. If there is a chance that I can use some of my outstanding vacation allowance against the notice period, I will do so. Basically I want to start as soon as possible.

ANSWER2: My last promotion put me on a ninety-day notice period where I could not work for any firm in the same industry for that period of time. Your firm is in a different industry so I am not sure that rule applies. I want to start as soon as possible so I may need to take some legal advice as to when I can.

ANSWER3: I am close to ending a project that should take another week to complete. The company really needs me to finish this and I feel honor bound not to leave them in the lurch. If I do that for them, they will release me from any notice period I have.

CHAPTER 8: INTERESTS OUTSIDE THE WORKPLACE

Introduction

Interviewers are keen that people enjoy a work life balance. You can just as easily build a network outside a workplace as inside. In addition, the more healthy your lifestyle, the more productive you will be. Speak freely about any clubs, societies, sports interest or charities that you are involved in. You may even find that you have some similar interests to the interviewer.

What are your outside interests?

ANALYSIS: There is no right answer to this question, and the wrong answer is that you watch TV all day! Outside interests can vary from sports, charitable fundraising to attending the theatre. Show her that you are motivated outside the work place.

ANSWER1: I like to channel some of professional experience into my charity work. I am an active fundraiser of XYZ.org and usually spend one Saturday morning each month running the committee, setting goals and monitoring achievements to date. It is good that I can use my skills outside the workplace for the benefit of those less fortunate.

ANSWER2: My kids have taken a keen interest in theatre and their interest has awoken my latent enthusiasm also. I am on the committee for the local amateur theatre where my role as bursar is to keep the theatre afloat and ensure that we can produce plays for the benefit of the community. Next year, I will be taking on the role of chairman.

ANSWER3: My father passed a few years ago from terminal cancer. Thankfully his illness was short lived but it was a horrendous shock to us all. I was spurred to action and have been an active event organizer for various cancer charities ever since. I find that both my academic and work experiences are very valuable in organizing and marketing events.

What do you do for fun?

ANALYSIS: They want to hear that you live a healthy lifestyle. Fun can be golf, tennis, swimming or playing with the kids. Work life balance is very important these days.

ANSWER1: I am a very keen golfer and although I am no Phil Mickelson, I do love getting out in the fresh air on a Saturday. It releases any latent tension and stress that builds up during the week. I truly believe that one is more productive with a fresh body and mind.

ANSWER2: I am real film buff and tend to go to the movie theatre twice a week if I can. My kids are at the age where I can bring them to matinees on Saturday afternoons. I find it great to switch off for a few hours. I also play an occasional game of tennis, weather permitting.

ANSWER3: My summer sport is outdoor jogging along the river. I tend to go at least three times a week while there is light. In the winter, my partner and I go to spinning classes at our local gym. We find it exhausting but the pain is worth is as we always feel on top of the world afterwards.

☙

Do you speak any other languages?

ANALYSIS: In some cases, this will be a prerequisite and you are likely to be tested in your proficiency. Usually job advertisements will specifically state if the company is looking for specific language skills. They may be asking you as they me see a fit for you further down the line in a foreign country or if you are open to learning further. Keep an open mind when answering this question. Your long-term career may depend on it.

ANSWER1: Yes, I am fluent in French and Spanish. In college I spent six months in Paris and another four in Madrid to perfect my skills. I have always gravitated towards learning new languages. Once I have commanded the basics, I find it quite easy to grasp a new language. One of the reasons, I applied for this role was due to the need for foreign language fluency.

ANSWER2: I have basic German and Italian; I am certainly not fluent in either but have been educated to a college standard. Should the need arise for me to perfect one of the languages with a view to a foreign assignment, then I do not believe that it would be a problem for me to brush up on the basics and take it to another level if necessary.

ANSWER3: No, I must confess that my focus in school or college was on engineering related subjects and so far in my career, this background has been very helpful. I am quick to learn and a very diligent student as you can see from my resume. I am not afraid to take on the challenge of learning a new language.

ご

Have you been inspired by any sporting figure?

ANALYSIS: You may or may not have been. The interviewers want to know what type of person influences you or whom do you see as a role model. It will raise some eyebrows if the person who influences you is a well know drug addict. The person does not necessary have to be a sports person either. Have a quality answer ready.

ANSWER1: The sporting figure who has inspired me to date is probably the worst golfer in the world, my Dad! Both my parents have made tremendous sacrifices to ensure that I received the best education they could afford and was exposed to many extracurricular activities. Both are very positive and have continuously inspired me over the years. I attribute my success to date to the values my parents have given me.

ANSWER2: Pele is the best soccer player in the world. He won many world cups and was simply a genius on the pitch. He was and continues to be a huge inspiration to me. However, the inspiration is mainly due to his off field activities. He has given so much back to the under privileged communities of the world and has never let fame get the better of him. Such balance is a huge inspiration.

ANSWER3: I don't really have one figure as such. But I find different aspects of many figures as inspirational. For example, I loved the tenacity and passion of John McEnroe. One thing I learned at an early age that you have to work hard to succeed in your sphere regardless of how much natural talent you think you have. All figures of inspirations have had their knocks, worked hard and continuously improved themselves through their respective careers.

∽

Are you involved in charity or community work?

ANALYSIS: Such involvement is always a positive on a resume and it will catch the eye of an interviewer. If you are not involved currently, it is not the end of the world or the interview. Interviewers are more interested in hearing that you understand the importance of giving back and that you do want to engage in such activity at some stage. This will impress on them that you are a team player.

ANSWER1: I consider myself very fortunate due to luck but mainly due to hard work. I am also very mindful that I was given the right platform to succeed. I ensure that I give something back to the community am a mentor to some inner city kids who do not have the same opportunity that I had.

ANSWER2: I am an active fundraiser for an international charity. I am on the events committee that organizes a sponsored run, golf outing and end of year dinner. I ensure that many of my work colleagues attend the event and our generous matching scheme promotes strong attendance. The events are also great for networking and sharing experiences with people from other industries.

ANSWER3: My current role demands that I travel constantly and as discussed this is one of the reasons why I am looking for a change. So in the last year, while I have made some charitable donations, I have not been able to actively participate as much as I want to. I intend to rectify this as soon as I get settled into a new role.

How can you channel external work activities into the workplace?

ANALYSIS: Positive energy is a great asset in the work place. If you participate in an external activity, it usually means that you enjoy it and gain from in both a physical and/or mental sense. Interviewers recognize this and they will expect you to recognize the benefits of external activity.

ANSWER1: I think that this can actually work both ways. I compliment my people network in the workplace with those outside. For example, I really enjoy playing golf at the weekends. When I set up a four ball, I always invite some from work and a friend from outside work. The discussions during the game often lead to deals or potential business opportunity.

ANSWER2: I am on the committee for the mini football league. Twenty teams of five participate in a round robin style tournament. About four hundred people attend to play and watch. My current company sponsors the event through my participation on the committee. We secure prime advertisement space and it is great exposure for the company. We always secure new and repeat business on account of this event.

ANSWER3: Yes definitely. You always represent your firm even when you are not in the office. In my mind, every event is a business networking opportunity. In addition, in this industry, the community is quite small so you have to be mindful of your reputation. I always use my external memberships to promote my company in the best light as I have seen people's extracurricular negative activities cause serious issues for them and their companies.

❦

What papers do you read?

ANALYSIS: Naturally, you can read anything you want. If there are industry specific magazines then there will be some expectancy that you keep in touch of industry and product develops. Also, at a macro level, you need to demonstrate that you are in tune with global economic and political events.

ANSWER1: I am an avid reader and likely to read pretty much anything in front of me! I read all the daily broad sheets as I feel it is imperative to keep up with the global economic and political situations. For industry specific details, I have some subscriptions to magazines that ensure that I keep up with industry regulations and launches.

ANSWER2: Given the advent of the Internet; I tend to do most of my reading online these days either from my phone or my PC. I find that the information is more real-time which is very important for this industry. With so much competition in this space, you cannot afford to miss some information that could put you behind the curve quickly.

ANSWER3: I like to mix up my reading between papers and the Internet. Aside from consolidating macro and geopolitical events, I enjoy reading the classifieds to find out what people are really looking for. There are numerous items that people list which gives me ideas for potential products. Online, I tend to read consumer blogs and review inventory movements to determine where the market is going.